MW01249080

ISBN 978-1-330-54932-2
PIBN 10077190

W. H. Treadway
New York City
7th February, 1890.

(Bac[illegible])
51

SERMONS

ON THE

LORD'S PRAYER.

By Rev. HENRY M. BACON,

PASTOR OF THE SECOND PRESBYTERIAN CHURCH,
COVINGTON, INDIANA.

AUBURN:
WILLIAM J. MOSES.
1854.

THE NEW YORK
PUBLIC LIBRARY
231147
ASTOR, LENOX AND
TILDEN FOUNDATIONS.
1903

THESE SERMONS

ARE AFFECTIONATELY DEDICATED

TO THE

Faithful and Generous Congregation,

TO WHOM THEY WERE PREACHED

BY THEIR GRATEFUL

PASTOR.

PREFACE.

No one reads a Preface: yet not to write one, would seem to argue stolid indifference, or overweening confidence, as to the success of his efforts, neither of which the author feels. He has, besides, a word or two to say for himself, to the reader of this book. If any are so impatient that they cannot sto to talk with him a moment, he cannot help it.

This book may be said to be printed, rather than published; for it is not supposed that it will fall into the hands of many who are not in some way acquainted with the author. It would be idle to weary any one with the reasons which have induced him thus to venture out from his retirement, in the very beginning, as it were, of his ministry. He cannot plead the novel and interesting apology, that he has been "urged," or even "solicited." He has taken the responsibility, and must abide by the consequences.

There are some things in this little volume, of which some who read it, perhaps many, may disapprove. The views here promulgated have not been rashly adopted. With a scanty Library, and few counsellors, the author has studied out for himself many of the results presented in these Discourses. He is satisfied that they are correct, and his prayer is, that if they are not, one effect of their publication may be his own conviction of his error. Criticism is neither deprecated nor defied. The author is too well aware of the many faults that even a careless eye can discover in these Sermons, not to know that he "who reads to criticise" will find plenty of employment. He does not think such captious fault-finding can ruffle the surface of his equanimity. At the same time, he will be grateful to those who will point out any errors, and thus help him to correct them.

These Sermons were preached in the early part of the summer of this year, andthis will explain some allusions to passing events, which have been left unchanged. The author had intended thoroughly to revise the whole, especially for the purpose of leaving out repetitions of the same thought in different sermons, but his health has not permitted him to accomplish the task. These repetitions are, the author thinks. appropriate to sermons actually preached to a congregation; for the business of the minister is to press upon his hearers, Sabbath after Sabbath, the same great truths. As they occur in this book, they may serve to remind the reader that he is to put himself in the position of a hearer.

If these Discourses shall lead any one to prize more highly the prayer our Lord taught us, the author will feel rewarded for his labor.

Covington, October, 1854.

CONTENTS.

CONTENTS.

PAGE

SERMON I.

SERMON II.

SERMON III.

SERMON IV.

SERMON V.

SERMON VI.

SERMON VII.

SERMON VIII.

SERMON IX.

SERMON I.

Our Father which art in Heaven.—Matt. 6 : 9.

I begin to day the fulfillment of a long cherished purpose. Years ago, the beauty and tenderness, the simplicity and comprehension of the Lord's Prayer attracted my attention, and they have grown upon me with every successive reading and repetition of it. Long before I had preached, or even sketched a sermon, I had made up my mind to devote a Course of Lectures to the exposition of this touching and instructive portion of our Savior's teachings. Many things have occurred from time to time to put off the accomplishment of this determination, till at last it seemed to be only a beautiful mirage, deluding and mocking me. I thank God that I have lived to begin this undertaking. May he spare us all to witness its conclusion. I shall be fully rewarded for my labor, if the views I present shall induce any mother, though irreligious herself, to teach her child this prayer, which our Lord taught us; if they shall lead any youth who has outgrown the teachings of pious parents, to repeat again these words of Him who spake as never man spake; or if, finally, (and certainly, I may hope for this reward,) they shall enable any disciple of Christ to cry more heartily and believingly, "Abba Father."

No more appropriate expression could have been chosen as the introduction to this prayer than the words, "Our Father." The Savior teaches us here at the outset the feelings with which we should approach God. We must draw nigh unto him as children to a father, for doubtless he is our Father. But let us analyze filial affection, and see what emotions enter into it as indispensable elements. First and foremost among these I place *reverence.* I know this virtue has nearly grown obsolete in our day. Generally, nay, almost universally, the child is the center around which the obsequious parents revolve, and to which the whole household gravitates. There is a sickly sentimentalism much in vogue in our times that would annihilate fear. I acknowledge that "'tis better far to rule by love than fear," but I maintain that a love in which there is no fear of offending, and no dread of just severity in consequence of offending, is a love that is not worth the having.

Reverence is an essential element of filial affection, and when it is wanting, that affection cannot exist in its highest and purest state.

The character of Him whom we call Our Father in Heaven, is eminently calculated to inspire this reverence. He is no such weak, indifferent being as some would imagine Him. He thundereth in the heavens He looketh on the earth, and it trembleth. His face is against them that do evil. Who would not fear this great and terrible God? I will not enlarge here upon this point, as our Savior has given us, in the very first petition of this prayer, an express and emphatic caution to beware of irreverence.

The second constituent of the feeling which children should cherish toward their parents, is *love*. Reverence and love, these are the prismatic rays, either of which alone is beautiful, but which when blended, as they always should be, illumine a home with clear and heavenly light.

Inspire your child with reverence and love for you, and you have done more for your mutual happiness, and for his success, than if you should give him the title deed to all the gold mines of California.

But let us turn our thoughts from our fathers, according to the flesh, to the Father of our spirits. We are to come to him with a trusting affection, and oh how much there is in his character to warrant and invite this: God is love. "Like as a father pitieth his children, so the Lord pitieth them that fear him." And it is the peculiar characteristic and crowning glory of the Christian religion, that it does thus reveal God as the object of child-like love. The Jew knew that God was awful; the Hindoo knows that God is to be dreaded; and even

> "The poor Indian, whose untutored mind
> Sees God in clouds and hears him in the wind,"

trembles before him. But it is the Christian into whose heart God sends forth his Spirit, crying Abba Father. Not that the Jews had no idea of God's paternal character. But this was by no means so clear and prominent as it is in the new dispensation. It is only since grace and truth have come by Jesus Christ, that we can boldly say, "Our Father who art in Heaven."

I have seen somewhere an allegory like this: A heathen knelt down to pray—a Jew passing by inquired, what do you call the Deity? He replied, the Destroyer; and asked in turn, what do you call him? The Almighty, was the answer. A Christian drew near and said, we call him Father; then they all knelt down together, saying, "Our Father who art in Heaven." And oh, what better bond of union could there be? Come, gay, thoughtless devotee of pleasure, come hard, heartless man of the world, come slave of Mammon, let us kneel down together and say, "Our Father who art in Heaven." Why should you be afraid? You are not: ah, why should you be ashamed to join your fellow men in asking your common Father for what you all need?

And this brings me to the second lesson which our Savior teaches us in this beginning of the Lord's prayer—the duty of social worship. Our Master here lays hold of, and appropriates to the service of religion, that great principle of associated action, the power of which men are just beginning to appreciate. Men undertake now to accomplish nothing by themselves; we must have a society for every thing. It has been heralded as one of the great discoveries of our time, that so much can be achieved in this way. But the Church of Christ was founded ages ago upon this basis, and is still held together by this bond.—Christians are formed into a society to effect a common purpose. To strengthen their own interest and to awaken that of others, they are to meet frequently and regularly. Masonry and Odd-Fellowship, with every phase and imitation of them, have borrowed this great principle from the Church. And in this we see the truth of the saying, that our Lord knew what was in man.—There is, too, in this adaptation of the Church to human nature, a convincing proof that they are from the same great Author.

But some one, willing to justify himself, and fighting against reason and revelation will say, "I do not need to join this society, to enter into this communion. I can be as good a Christian out of the Church as in it." No, my friend, you cannot. You may be a Christian out of the Church: you may be a better Christian than some in it: but you cannot be as good a one out of it as you would be in it. Your child may be a scholar by studying at home: he may be a better scholar than some who go to school; but he cannot be as good a scholar, as with the same application he would have been, if he had been brought, under the care of a competent instructor, into daily contact and rivalry with those pursuing the same studies. It is not simply because it is cheaper and just as easy for one teacher to instruct twenty children as five, that we gather our youth into schools: but there is great benefit in association, in friendly strifes, in the action and re-action of one mind upon another. It may be that the affiliated states of this great confederacy would be prosperous and powerful, if sundered and left each to stand alone; but we all know that they could not be as safe as they now are, bound together in one happy union.—In union there is strength: and you must not say you can be as good a Christian out of the Church as in it.

But there are some who say, "I can worship God at home as well as in the church. It will do me more good to read an excellent sermon at home than to listen to an ordinary one in the church." I have even found professors of religion, who would thus undervalue that public worship which was one of the great purposes for which the Church was instituted. Granting that you can, (let me say to any such who may happen to hear me,) derive more instruction from reading at home alone, our Savior teaches us in this introduction to the Lord's prayer, the necessity of social, in distinction from individual, worship. You must meet with your fellow men and say, "Our Father who art in Heaven." You have social blessings which can be properly acknowledged only in a social capacity; and I deny that you can worship God as well by yourself as with your fellow men. This is the very mistake of monks and nuns. You forget, or else this thing you are willingly ignorant of, that there is no one of the faculties and feelings of man, that can attain to maturity and perfection, except amid the intercourse and the influence of society. This is a fundamental law of our being, which can neither be violated nor evaded; and religion is subject to it. If you would have submission, reverence, love, faith, all the feelings that are called into exercise in the worship of God, possess and overwhelm your soul, you must meet with the great congregation,

"Where sorrow flows from eye to eye,
And joy from heart to heart."

If you would have the great truths of the gospel sink deep into your heart, you must see the tear stealing down the cheek of the sorrowing penitent, you must watch the light of hope as it breaks over the beclouded face of some despairing sinner. Heaven is no such secluded solitude as you would seek. John saw there a multitude whom no man could number, and their voice was as the sound of many waters. If you would anticipate heaven, you must go with the multitude who keep holy day. And in saying this, I underrate or discourage private worship, no more than our Savior did in teaching us to say, *Our* Father. In the beginning of this chapter he tells us to go into our closets and shut to our doors, and pray to our Father who seeth in secret; thus plainly teaching us the necessity of secret prayer. Here he shows, indirectly it is true, but none the less plainly, that we are to engage in social worship. And this is the order of nature; secret prayer is the first in the order of time and of importance. Every one should prepare in the closet for the public worship of God. Without this preparation, it is almost impossible to render acceptable worship. Certainly I should have more charity for one who, with mistaken views, neglected the public services of God's house, than for one who deserted his closet. Yet nothing can take the place of public, social worship. It exerts upon the heart of the believer an important and a peculiar influence; its influence upon society, too, is incalculable and indispensable. Deprive this community of all the public services of religion, and it would, slowly perhaps, but surely slide back into the ignorance and cruelty of savage life. The preaching of the gospel, the voice of prayer and praise, restrain men who never hear them; and who shall estimate their influence over the worldly-minded and irreligious, who habitually frequent the courts of the Lord's house? To the mere philanthropist, our Sabbath gatherings should have a deep interest. Here, as the rich and the poor meet together, will they not feel that the Lord is the maker of them both?

And this leads me to observe that in this introduction, our Lord teaches us the common brotherhood of the race. The plain and repeated inculcation of this truth, is one of the distinguished and distinguishing peculiarities of the Christian religion. The religion of Paganism, both ancient and modern, were state and national, designed for a single race, making little or no effort to extend their influence beyond certain limits. The same is true, though perhaps not to so great an extent, of the Jewish religion. But when our Savior came, he boldly told his disciples that their field was the world. He sent them out into all the world, to preach the gospel to every creature; and they did so, to the Greek and to the Jew, to the Barbarian and the Scythian, to the bond and the free. And they showed how all social distinctions melted away in the glance of the Lord. They preached with equal plainness and fervor to the jailer, in their dungeon, and to Agrippa in the audience chamber of Kings; to the barbarous people of the island of Melita, and to them of Cæsar's household.

Christianity, where it has not degenerated into a miserable caricature, still teaches that God has made of one blood all nations of men. It recognizes no inferior race, so feeble, so debased, as to be out of the circle of its sympathies. Wherever the Christian finds a human body wrapped round a human soul, he finds a brother with whom he can kneel down and say—"Our Father in Heaven." It is upon this broad principle that the structure of Foreign Missions is built, and all the pert witticisms of modern philosophers and "reformers" cannot shake it. How puny do their achievements appear, compared with the world-embracing charities of that army of the Lord of Hosts, which goes not with the war of artillery, or the gleam of the bayonet, but with the Bible and the Sabbath School, to wipe away the tears and heal the wounds of the whole family of man.

But our Savior does not here teach us to sympathize with and care only for the stranger with whom we have no dealings, though he surely includes all such among the children of our Father in Heaven. But this brotherly feeling is to control our daily life. He who prays after this manner cannot be scornful or selfish. Come, proud, haughty professor of religion, come, envious, malignant disciple of Christ, (O, strange contradiction in terms,) kneel down in the morning, and say, "Our Father." Can you despise or slight your fellow men, because they are not dressed according to your taste? Can you talk bitterly and reproachfully of them, because they do not pay as much attention to you, and are not as intimate with you as you desire: not remembering that in estimating your own merits, you are apt to err in your own favor? Cold, heartless, avaricious man, kneel down at night by the side of that bed on which you expect the Lord to keep you while you sleep, and as you say, "Our Father who art in Heaven," think of the poor whose faces you have ground, or the widow from whom you have taken her children's bread. Severe, harsh, unrelenting judge of the wayward and the heedless, remember that this erring one is your brother or your sister. I do not hesitate to say that no one can imbibe the spirit of this beginning of the Lord's prayer, without being, in the best and highest sense of the word, a philanthropist. Let the principle taught here pervade all hearts, and it would revolutionize society. Trickery and deceit, harshness and oppression, would be banished from the earth.

But if any where this feeling should govern, it is in the intercourse of fellow Christians, both of the same and of different denominations. Doubtless, God is our Father, in a peculiar sense. We are fellow-citizens with the saints, and of the household of God. We are heirs of God, and joint heirs with Christ. Shall we bite and devour one another? Shall we be jealous and suspicious of each other? Let there be no strife between us, for we are brethren. Let us love as brethren; then shall the world behold how good and how pleasant it is for brethren to dwell together in unity. And nothing will help us to do this more than worshiping together, saying in unison, "Our Father who art in heaven." I disapprove entirely of the conduct of some professors of religion, who never go to Church when they do not have preaching in their own house, or at least by their own minister. Thus keeping yourself aloof from, and ignorant of your fellow Christians, how can you learn to love them? I have read, somewhere, of a man who went out with his gun in a valley. Amid the gray fog of the early dawn, he saw something move before him, which he took to be a wild beast. As he raised his gun to fire, it occurred to him that it would be well to be more sure of its character. As he climbed the mountain, and drew nearer, the light increasing, the vapor melted away, and he saw it was a man. And when he came close up to him, he found it was his brother.

So you, my fellow Christian, while you stay down amid the mists of bigotry and prejudice, may shrink away from some fancied monster; but climb higher up the mount of God: let the light of the Sun of Righteousness pour its radiance around and into your heart. You shall find he whom you dreaded is a man, a man of like passions with yourself; and when you come to see him as he is, you shall clasp him to your heart, a brother beloved. And nothing, I say again, will help us to cultivate such a feeling, more than worshiping together. We shall then feel that we have one Lord, one faith, one baptism, for we are all baptized into Christ. We do all eat of the same spiritual meat, and do all drink of the same spiritual drink. We shall feel, also, how many and intimate are the ties that bind us together—having a common Father, loving and trusting the same Savior, heirs of the same heavenly inheritance, pilgrims to the same dear home.

And this brings me to the final lesson of this

introduction,—that heaven is our home. We should therefore set our affections in heaven, where Christ sitteth, at the right hand of God. Worldly-minded professor of religion, hasting to be rich, so engrossed by the pursuit of wealth that you find no time to turn aside into your closet, or to drop into the prayer-meeting; overtasking yourself so much that the Sabbath finds you too weary to really enjoy its delightful services; thoughts of gain stealing on amid its quiet hours, to cast their dark, forbidding shadow o'er the

"Sweet fields beyond the swelling flood,"

what an ungrateful, or, at least, heedless child you are.

Why do you so seldom turn to your home high up in heaven? Why do you not lay up your treasure there? Ah, where your treasure is, your heart will be also. On the other hand, my brother, are you poor, compelled to toil for daily bread? Is your home scantily furnished, and your food coarse, while the proud and haughty around you are clothed in purple and fine linen, and fare sumptuously every day? Oh, my brother, this is but a way-side inn, where we tarry for a night. In our Father's house are many mansions. One who loves us better than we love ourselves, has gone before to prepare a place for us.

A home in heaven, what a joyful thought, as the poor man toils in his weary lot! Have you deeper sorrows than poverty or suffering can bring, some hidden wound healed over outwardly, yet festering and bleeding within: that bitterness which every heart knows only for itself? Lift up your eyes and rejoice, for your redemption draweth nigh. There the wicked cease from troubling, and the weary are at rest.

"His own soft hand shall wipe the tears
From every weeping eye;
And pains and groans, and griefs and fears,
Shall cease eternally."

"Oh, who would live alway, away from his God,
Away from yon heaven, that blissful abode:
Where the rivers of pleasure flow o'er the bright plains,
And the noontide of glory eternally reigns."

SERMON II.

Hallowed be thy name : Matt. 6 : 9.

"BEHOLD what manner of love the Father hath bestowed upon us, that we should be called the sons of God." The fact that God permits us to call him "Our Father," might well overjoy us. To chasten and restrain us, lest in the exuberance of our gladness we should forget the awful majesty which invests the Divine character, our Lord teaches us, at the outset, to say, as our first petition, "Hallowed be thy name." We learn from this that it is of the first importance that, in all our approaches to God, while we come with the confidence and simplicity of children, we are always to draw nigh, even in the full assurance of our faith, "with reverence and Godly fear."

We are taught here, in the first place, that all our direct addresses to God, which might be strictly called the use of his name, should be pervaded by awful solemnity. There is, in the prayers of some really good men, at times, a blasphemous familiarity, which is absolutely shocking. Such persons, in their mistaken zeal to be like children coming to a father, forget how holy and reverend is the name of God, and they assume, in their prayers, the free and easy style of the bar-room and the theatre. This is not only to be regretted, but must be strongly condemned and strenuously resisted. The application to God of endearing epithets, of a familiar and common character, addressing him as if he were altogether such an one as ourselves, is so abhorrent to reason as well as Revelation, that I need not enlarge upon it here. It is sufficient to call your attention to it, and thus put you upon your guard against a sad mistake, into which some good men have fallen.

But there is an evil akin to this, to which we are all exposed, and I think it quite important to refer to it. It is a mechanical, thoughtless repetition of God's name in our prayers. This is a taking the name of God in vain, which we should be careful to avoid. That we often repeat the name of God in our devotions, when it is unnecessary and out of place, may seem a slight matter, not worthy to be spoken of here; but everything connected with the character and glory of God is of the utmost importance. Especially should everything about our worship show a deep and absorbing reverence for the Lord our God. While this is true of all worship, it is peculiarly so of our public services; for these are designed, as has been remarked, to have, and do have a great influence upon the irreligious. We should take pains, therefore, to have the public worship of God impress even the thoughtless listener with at least a belief in our holy fear of the high and lofty One, if that emotion may not steal imperceptibly into their souls.

And this naturally leads me to remark, that this petition, "Hallowed be thy name," is by no means to be restricted to any such narrow, literal interpretation as would make it refer only to the use of God's name. There are, at times, large portions of our prayers in which we do not need to make formal mention of the name of God; and we ought, as has already been remarked, to avoid all unnecessary repetition of it: but even those portions are to be pervaded by a subdued earnestness, that will show to God, and to our fellow men, that we do not forget that He is in heaven, and we are upon the earth. Every intelligent reader of Scripture knows, that God's name is often put for his character,—the full assemblage of his attributes. In teaching us thus at the very beginning to pray—"Hallowed be thy name," our Lord shows us that humility and reverence should pervade and control all our prayers, and every part of them. All attempts at display, whether by ambitious ornament or learned discourse, are here sadly out of place. Do we not sometimes find, among ministers and those who are often called upon to lead in public prayer, a disposition to impress upon their fellow worshipers an idea of their happy use of language, the depth of their humility, or the correctness of their theology, rather than an absorbing reverence for God, and a consciousness of guilt and want? Such a spirit, in the performance of public worship, defeats the object of its institution, for it can never produce its proper effect upon the devout or the undevout, except when it is, and is felt to be, a simple, childlike pouring out of our hearts before God. Once allow people to suppose that you are praying to them, and you might as well drop even the form of addressing God.

You will often see a disposition to criticise the devotional efforts of Christians, which is equally at war with the teachings of this petition, and the spirit of true worship. I have repeatedly heard persons, when going home from prayer-meeting, thoughtlessly—I had almost said profanely,—comparing the prayers of different individuals. Such persons would do well to remember that they are perhaps not very good judges as to who makes the best prayer. Often, in the eye of God, the fluent, eloquent man, is guilty of solemn mockery, while he who utters only a few, incoherent words, pressed out of a broken, contrite heart, goes down to his house justified, rather than the other. I hope none of you, my

Christian brethren, will indulge in this foolish, unchristian criticism, and that none of you will be troubled or frightened by it. Do not bc kept from the prayer-meeting and its duties, because you cannot deliver to your fellow-Christians a polished oration. I, for one, would much rather that, overwhelmed by a sense of your own vileness and littleness in the sight of God, you should not so much as lift up your eyes unto heaven, and should utter only a few, simple words, than that you should stand up with undisturbed composure, and voluble self-complacence, to pour out your fiue-turned phrases. I do not disparage case and fluency in prayer. They are desirable, and we should endeavor to acquire them, while we should carefully avoid an incoherent, fragmentary method of prayer. But do not seek the honor that comes from man; and do not be kept from praying to God by a fear, that you will not receive honor of man.

I have intimated that ease and propriety in prayer is a matter of study and acquisition. I need not stop to prove this, since we all acknowledge that the days of direct inspiration have long since passed, and that whatever excellence we obtain, is the result of labor and practice. Instead, then, of absenting yourself from the prayer-meeting, or sitting down in contented indolence and carelessness, because you have not what is called the "gift of public prayer," you ought rather to cultivate a devotional spirit, in your closet and family circle, assured that out of the abundance of the heart the mouth will speak. Study the prayers of inspired men, as given to us in the word of God. Especially, endeavor to conform your prayers to that one which we are now considering, given to us expressly as a model,—for he says, "after this manner pray ye,"—by Him who spake as never man spake. You would also derive great assistance from the works of some uninspired Christians, such as Henry, Watts, Scott and Jay, who have either written for our instruction, or have given us forms adapted to our various wants and peculiarities. I must be permitted to add, here, that I know of no better uninspired model, of the solemn tenderness and brief simplicity which should characterize our prayers, than the Liturgy of the Protestant Episcopal Church. No one can really engage in public worship, as conducted in these forms, without having his heart subdued to the same tone of affectionate reverence. This may seem positively heretical to some, who have been accustomed to look upon the use of forms in worship as dangerous, and indeed wicked. But this ground is utterly untenable. There is no Church that is entirely without forms. In our present condition, it would be impossible to do without them. That is to say, worship, and public worship especially, must be conducted upon some plan, according to some regular method. Our forms are simple, and variable within wide limits, at the pleasure of the officiating minister. The forms of our Episcopal brethren are more elaborate and invariable. The clergyman cannot alter, —indeed, it is doubtful whether he can omit, any part of the prescribed ritual. It is our form, our method of worship, to use extemporary prayers, while it is theirs to repeat prayers composed beforehand for the occasion. The question between them and us is one of expediency, whether their mode of conducting public worship is preferable to ours. We do not think it sinful for them to use written forms of prayer; but we hold that extemporary prayer is best calculated to cultivate a devotional spirit, and we protest especially against being confined to an invariable phraseology.

It is not my duty, now, to enter into the discussion of that subject; if it were, I think I could show that our views are correct. One thing I would suggest to any one, who may dislike my commending the Liturgy of the Episcopal Church, as a model in some respects. Such forms of prayer, when we are not tied to them, and do not cling to them with superstitious reverence, may be of great use. He who cannot pray without them, in his family, for instance, had better employ them. A book of prayers, a veritable "Prayer-Book," compiled by 180 ministers of Scotland, has been published by a Presbyterian house, and warmly commended by Presbyterian periodicals; and I have no doubt that he who is slow of speech, and has little of the gift of prayer, would derive great assistance from studying and occasionally employing such forms. It is for this reason that I commend to you the Episcopal Liturgy: especially the forms for Morning and Evening prayer—not because I approve of every thing in it. There are expressions in the baptismal and ordination services, which every Protestant must regret as unfortunate, to say the least; and in the ordinary Sabbath services, the general tenor of which is so unexceptionable, and to me so lovely and impressive, the declaration of absolution has always grated harshly on my ear. But the individual prayers themselves are, I say again, among the best of uninspired models—the finest specimens of what a prayer should be. There is such an entire absence of display, or straining after effect; such simple grandeur, such entire forgetfulness of ourselves breathes in every line, that it is refreshing to turn to them in these days, when pride and bombast seem to be invading the holiest of holies, when we intercede with God. I do not think you could read or hear them in a proper frame of mind, without being benefited.

But some of you may say, this has not been your experience. You have occasionally attended the Episcopal Church, but the services always seemed dull and unmeaning. The sermon may have made an impression upon you, but the worship never seemed to do you any good. The reason of this is, that you did not conform to their modes of worship. You did not endeavor to enter into the spirit of the occasion, and to actually worship with them. This you should have done, just as when you go to the Methodist Church, you are to worship according to their forms. And you are not to suppose that, because the forms are different from those you are accustomed to, that therefore it is not worship, and that you are not bound to regard it as such. You have no more right to treat the worship of Episcopalians with contempt or indifference, because they read or recite their prayers, than they have to despise ours, because we pray without the use of such forms. When either of you come to a place of worship as a critic or a spectator, you do not hallow the name of our Father in heaven as we here confess that we should, and pray that we may. These forms will do you good, if you use them lawfully; and perhaps some of you, who shrink from them with a horror as superstitious as the reverence with which others cling to them, would be the very ones to be most benefited by their occasional use.

There is probably no part of the worship of God in which there is so little hallowing of the name of God, as in singing his praise. How often do persons, even in the sanctuary, join in these solemn ascriptions of devout homage to the King of glory, with the same flippant carelessness with which they would sing a love-ditty or a negro melody. Indeed, you will sometimes hear them, when engaged in worldly business or pleasure, sing with wild hilarity, or even uproarious mirth, such sacred words as,

> "Before Jehovah's awful throne,"

or,

> "Alas and did my Savior bleed!"

It chills me with horror to hear any one thus sporting with these awful themes. God is expressly declared by inspiration itself to be fearful in praises, and we should no more trifle with these songs of adoration, than with the prayers that are offered to him. I know that the department of worship we are now considering has its peculiarities. It is associated with music, an art which requires study, and which has attractions of its own, entirely independent of the devout emotion to be expressed. I am far from condemning practice, preparative for conducting the praise of God in the public assembly. Study is as necessary for this as for preaching; and direct inspiration is no more to be relied upon in the one case than in the other. There are, however, some things in relation to this part of worship, which I think it important and appropriate to mention in this connection. In the first place, I am from principle opposed to the use of hymns and sacred songs in teaching music. This will seem to some a superstitious strictness about little matters, like the unwillingness which many feel, and I confess myself one of them, to have political meetings, concerts, and similar gatherings held in a church. But nothing is trivial which concerns the cultivation of reverence for our Heavenly Father. And the practice in question has such a natural and necessary tendency to make the name and attributes of God seem common and worthless, that I do not see how the religious have tolerated it so long. No one at all sensitive as to the employment of words, endeared as many of these are to the pious heart, can visit a singing school in full blast, without being grieved at the nonchalant manner in which they are sung, and the style in which their execution is criticised. Train up a child to such a use of the name of God and his praises, and it is almost impossible to teach him properly to reverence them.

I trust the time is not far distant, when a thorough reform will be effected on this point.

It has been intimated that practice is necessary to prepare for public worship. The use of sacred words is of course allowable at such times, for the end in view can often be attained in no other way. But you should be very cautious in their employment. Never forget the solemnity of the words you use, and the awful grandeur of the Being to whom they are addressed. While I would not insist, and perhaps ought not to, that in such meetings there should be the sobriety of worship, yet I must say that all frivolity and buffoonery are intolerable and abominable to God and man. Scenes are sometimes witnessed in such gatherings as these, that are shocking in the extreme. Let every Christian, to whom God has given the priceless gift of song, set himself against these enormities. Let him remember that the music of earth, weak and faint though it be, is akin to that of Heaven; and let him imagine how the romp and the jester would appear amid that "multitude whom no man can number."— Especially when actually engaged in worship, should we be careful to hallow the name of God. Let your soul be full of devout reverence. Be more anxious to worship the Lord in the beauty of holiness, than to win applause or to escape the chagrin of failure. And let me add here, that ridicule or contempt, or anything resembling them, are just as inappropriate to mistakes made in singing the praise of God, as they are, and are acknowledged to be, to mistakes made in prayer. We are not here as mere spectators of a musical entertainment, critics of an artistic performance. He who would thus degrade the public worship of God, knows nothing of the awful sublimity which attaches itself to the meanest conventicle, the scantiest assemblage. "Where two or three are gathered together in my name, there am I in the midst of them," said He who fills immensity with his presence, and whose throne is in the heaven of heavens. We are here before God, all praying, while but one voice is heard, all praising, while but a few sing. "Would God that all the Lord's people were prophets, and that the Lord would put his Spirit upon them."

This petition teaches us to avoid, and we pray in it that we may avoid every thing like contempt or neglect of any part of the worship of God. Talking, laughing, reading, lounging, and gazing about, are, as I have often declared, notorious offences against the simplest rules of good breeding. You may know when you see a person indulging in any of these, that he has been very poorly instructed, or has paid but little attention to what he was taught. But I arraign these practices now upon a charge of much greater enormity. They are insults to the infinite majesty of God. They are slights, put not upon the preacher, but upon the gospel which he preaches. "He that despiseth you, despiseth me," said He who commanded us to go and preach the gospel. In other places, and when engaged in other labors, I can endure the whispering and other disturbances of the ill-bred and the silly, but when I come to the Sanctuary, clothed with the authority of an ambassador for God, I should be false to my solemn vows, and to every feeling of my heart, did I not demand for the message of the Lord the profound silence of a thoughtful attention. He who hallows the name of our Father in heaven, will be sure to accord it.

There is a way of showing disrespect for the worship of God which I must notice briefly. It is true, and I am happy to bear this testimony, we as a congregation are seldom interrupted in this way, but the practice in question is common in places, and it is well to have correct views in regard to it. He who stalks out of the house of God with an air of defiance or contempt during the progress of worship, declares as plainly as if he asserted it in words, that these services are a mere idle spectacle, which he can leave whenever he is weary. Need I say that this view is erroneous? The worship of God is a solemn duty, which every one of us is bound to perform, and he who disturbs the pious worshiper, is not only guilty of a gross breach of politeness, but he turns his back upon the God in whose hands his breath is, and whose are all his ways. Another form of disrespect common among us, I only allude to. There are many persons who are unwilling to kneel down during family prayer. This may seem a slight matter, but it is important as a token of the person's state of mind.—He is ashamed to have his fellow men know that he humbles himself before God ; yet what posture more proper for him to assume? If he had any sense of the terrible majesty of God and his own weakness, if he hallowed the name of our Father in heaven as he should, would he refuse this feeble tribute of reverence?

The disposition for which we pray in this petition will throw a halo of sacredness around every thing connected with the worship of God, the places and times in which it is performed, the scenes with which it is associated. Many good people, who would not for the world be guilty of any indecorous conduct during the progress of worship, will yet indulge in foolish, giddy conversation and even laughter, before the services commence and after they are over. I do not believe there should be anything sour or forbidding about the worship of God. A word or two of cheerful conversation is not out of place ; but this mirth seems to me almost profane, when we are just about to call upon God, or when the solemn impressions that should have been made upon us, have had neither time nor opportunity to be effaced. Especially does this trouble me at the close of worship. I can bear with those who, coming in with their minds all unprepared for the sacred scenes of the Lord's day and the Lord's house, their thoughts wandering like the fool's eyes to the ends of the earth,—I can bear with them, if they do not hallow the name of God But how can people laugh and talk so carelessly when the solemn words they have heard or uttered have hardly had time to die out of their ears? I speak of this more in sorrow than in anger, for I have often been grieved in this way, and sometimes in this very house. There is also not unfrequently a haste in leaving the house of God which must affect the devout worshiper unpleasantly. The concluding moments of service are dedicated to the looking up of hats, the arranging of dresses, the opening of pew doors, and securing a fair start in the race from the sanctuary. All this strikes me as very unseemly. It appears to be saying with them of old, "what a weariness is it, when will the Sabbath be over?" I greatly admire the custom of our Episcopal brethren, for all the congregation to wait devoutly a moment or two before they stir from their places. It is only a form, you will say. I grant it, but it is a form eminently calculated to manifest and to suggest the reverence we should always feel and exhibit in the worship of God.

We have hitherto been considering only distinct and formal acts of worship. Is the spirit of this petition to be limited to these? It will require but little consideration to see that we here pray that a deep and hearty reverence for our Father in heaven may be breathed into every part of our life. What confidence can we have, to say nothing of God, who looks on the heart, in the piety of him who kneels at the altar, or covers his face in the sanctuary, and goes forth to blaspheme, or to talk lightly of God? It must be evident that the perjurer, however exact he may be in the performance of his devotions, does not hallow the name of God. Upon this point, of course, you who are present need no instruction. But did it ever occur to you that the manner in which oaths are commonly administered and taken, has little of the solemnity befitting such a transaction? An oath is a solemn appeal to the Almighty, to attest the truth of what we are about to utter—the faithfulness with which we will discharge the duties upon which we are about to enter. Can a man who has any proper sense of the majesty of "Him with whom we have to do," make such a declaration with the recklessness which is often witnessed in our courts of justice, and at the inauguration of officers. A reform in this matter is greatly needed. And we, my Christian friends, when called upon to participate in any such transaction, are the ones to begin it.

It would be well if, into the lips at least of public speakers, and especially those who discuss political topics, could be instilled this spirit of reverence. The name of God is a favorite expletive with them; it is always introduced wherever it will round a period, or produce a sensation. Their frequent appeals to "the Great Supreme" betray, through the mock solemnity with which they are thinly veiled, their utter indifference to the Lord, our God. I would as soon hear the profane jest and coarse blasphemy of the gambler and the loafer, as these devout expressions falling so heartless from the lips of one whose daily life proclaims that God is not in all his thoughts. Yet pious people! they are shocked at the one, while they smile on the other. Have they so little discernment as not to perceive that these irreligious, and sometimes vicious men, have stolen the livery of the court of heaven, if not to serve the devil, at least to serve themselves. I apprehend that the real difficulty is, that they are so little in the habit of hallowing the name of God in their own every day life, that the mere idle use of it, if it sounds well, if it does not absolutely force itself upon them as outrageously blasphemous, passes unnoticed, or awakens but little emotion. There is often, in the ordinary conversation of truly pious people, and sometimes even in their religious discourse, a careless way of speaking the name of God, against which I must protest. You will hear them talk, for instance, of "God's heavens," and "God's world," in a tone and manner which shows that they do not reverence him as they should, and that they have little idea that heaven is his throne, and the earth is his footstool.

It is related of Queen Elizabeth, that she never spoke the name of God without pausing a moment to show that she hallowed it, and oftener than otherwise she would say, "God, my Maker," so deeply did she seem to feel her dependence upon him. There are some of us, perhaps, who count ourselves much more pious than this haughty monarch, who would do well to copy her example. I would not go as far as the Jews, who counted the word Jehovah, the proper name of God, too sacred to be uttered, and even when it occurred in reading the Scriptures, substituted another word in its place. But let us at all times hallow the name of our Father in heaven, never mentioning him or any of his attributes but with becoming reverence.

Before dismissing this particular topic, I would call your attention to a singular circumstance which, in my judgment, shows a want of reverence for the name of God. Many pious people put this "fearful and glorious name" on a level with that of the devil, and such words as hell, damnation, and the like. Now the use of such expressions in idle banter, or in moments of passion, is profane and wicked. These people, who are so reckless in their conversation, show that they have no very strong conviction of the existence of a fallen spirit who is "not less than archangel ruined." Nor can they have even a faint idea of the "indignation and wrath, tribulation and anguish," which God will visit upon every soul of man that doeth evil. But this careless use of such phrases is not for a moment to be considered as of equal guilt with the reckless and blasphemous mention of the name of God, and especially of that worthy name by the which we are called, the name of Jesus, at which every knee should bow, and every tongue confess. Let this latter stand alone on its own bad eminence.

The same general principle, which I have laid down in regard to our use of God's name, applies to his word. "Thou hast magnified thy word," says the Psalmist, "above all thy name." This is generally understood by commentators as referring to the promise of the Messiah. But may it not mean also that the Bible is the clearest and highest revelation of his character, God has ever made to man; that while some indistinct and disconnected lessons might be spelled out from what is called the book of nature, it is only in the word of God, that he who runs can read? It seems to me that if "an undevout astronomer is mad," an undevout possessor of the Bible is much more so. If it is what it claims to be, the direct voice of God to man, it should be heard with the utmost reverence. Especially, my Christian friends, should we be careful in our treatment of the Scriptures, in which we think we have eternal life, never to quote them in jest, never speak of or allude to them lightly. Do not suffer this to be done in your presence ordinarily without rebuke. They are the word of the living God, which must not be trifled with.

As I remarked in reference to actual worship, that not only prayer and praise, but every part of the service, and everything connected with it, should be instinct with reverence; so now I would say, as to our every day life, that all these things should be spoken of and treated with due respect. Many, I fear a great many, professors of religion, have a jocose way of talking about the worship of God. Preaching, praying, asking a blessing, conversing with the thoughtless or the unawakened, are topics, over which they make merry among themselves. Indeed, I grieve to say, I have sometimes heard them do this with the ungodly and the profane. And when such people come to speak of the rites and forms of those who differ somewhat from themselves, they assume a sneering and contemptous tone, or at least they manifest a bitter and fault-finding spirit. My brethren, I must publicly protest against this. Whatever you may think of it, I am persuaded that in the eye of God it is profanity. It is taking the name of the Lord in vain. If a man really felt that reverence for God and his service, for which we pray in this petition, could he trifle with such sacred themes, as many professedly Christian people do? Suffer me to caution you especially against treating the forms of other Churches contemptuously. I am, for instance, often grieved at the coarse jokes and sneering words of very good people in regard to immersion. And I single this out, because I think profane language in regard to it more common among us than in reference to any other rite. I know how we are provoked and irritated. I am aware how much they revile our practice. I bring against them no railing accusation, but say to every such reviler, "The Lord rebuke thee." We must remember, however, that their sin is no excuse for ours. Indeed, we have less reason for such language than they, for while they do not admit the validity of our form, we do that of theirs. Let us never forget, that in administering immersion, they are really performing a solemn act of worship, an ordinance of the Lord's house, though in our judgment they put themselves to unnecessary trouble, and insist too much upon the mere form of the rite. And so of every other observance of our fellow-Christians, to which we are not accustomed, or of which we disapprove.

But we do not simply pray for ourselves in this petition. As in the beginning of the prayer we include the whole world in its embrace, so here we ask God to put an end to all superstition and idolatry; that all false religions and all corruptions of the true religion may be banished from the earth; that the name of God may be one, and his praise one, from the rising of the sun to the going down of the same. We pray that perjury, with its false lips on the word of God, and its murderous hand lifted to heaven, may be driven back into the bottomless pit from whence it came. We pray that no longer, as we walk the streets and mingle with our fellow men, shall our cars be saluted with oaths and blasphemy; that never again may a creature of God stand up amid his works, crowned with mercy and loving kindness, to insult the awful Majesty of "the Great Supreme;" that everywhere the Church of Christ, and the ordinances thereof, may be treated with proper respect, nay, be loved and enjoyed. What pious heart will not pray, "Hallowed be thy name."

——"Oh may the hour soon come,
When all false gods, false creeds, false prophets,
Allowed in thy good pleasure for a time,
Demolished, the great world shall be at last
The mercy-seat of God, the heritage
Of Christ, and the possession of the Spirit,
The Comforter, the Wisdom."

SERMON III.

Thy Kingdom Come.—Matt. 6 : 10.

From the days of the Grecian sages until now, men have disputed the question, "What is the best form of government?" The great majority of the wise and good have preferred the democratic or republican. And there are, of course, none of us of a contrary opinion. But there are certain limitations of this verdict, which we ought not to forget. All are not qualified to live under, or at least to have a voice in a republic. This applies, of course, not only to individuals, but to nations. Who would set up a republic among the Hottentots or Bushmen of South Africa? What folly in the American Missionaries, or the earlier adventurers to the Sandwich Islands, to have dethroned the king and proclaimed a democracy? But now, by a long course of training, protracted through years, they are fitted for a republican form of government, and are now asking admission into this great confederacy.

A free government is, in its last analysis, self-government. It is no poetic or legal fiction, to say that in this country people govern themselves.

They do this not merely in an indirect and metaphorical way, by electing those who make and execute the laws, but literally, and directly, by voluntarily submitting to those laws. If they did not, how else could they be executed, since there is no kingly power or standing army to compel obedience? And what is to hinder us from electing those who will connive at, or aid in our disobedience? Indeed, we have seen in a sister state, where men do not thus govern themselves, but give themselves up to the violence of unbridled passion, that they ride triumphant over the prostrate laws, and defy the state and national government. If they do this in the green tree, what shall be done in the dry? If such a state of things can exist in a little borough, with the power of the state and national governments, and the social omnipotence of public opinion arrayed against it, what would become of us if the same lawless spirit pervaded the entire country? Again, I say, the people do govern themselves.

The people of France have repeatedly shown themselves incapable of this self-government, thus paving the way for those usurpations which have of late so often disgraced her history, though by no means excusing, and far less justifying the perjury and treachery by which they have been accomplished.

France, said one who knew her well, when in

the time of her last revolution he heard some persons wishing she had a Washington—"France needs not a Washington, but a people." The same may be said of the southern republics of this continent, they need a people—a people accustomed to, and in the practice of self-government. Democratic institutions are weak and unsteady among them, or have been supplanted by despotism, not because there are no persons among them capable of wielding the power and directing the destinies of a republic, nor yet because there are no persons qualified to live under such a government; but they are too few and far scattered to control the turbulent and the ignorant. There are not enough of them to make a people. There is a populace, a rabble, to be bought and sold, to be coaxed and terrified; but no people to govern themselves. We live quietly and prosperously under a republic, not because every man is capable of voting intelligently, and understanding the great questions at issue before the country; not because all reverence the sacred majesty of the law, and submit to it for its own sake. This is notoriously untrue; nor yet because, according to a recent doctrine, God has taken the Sabbath-breakers and profane swearers, who fill the high places of our land, under his protection. But there is such a proportion of intelligent, upright, moral men, that they over-rule and govern the rest. Let ignorance and passion gain the ascendency, and the sun of our liberty will go down in a sea of anarchy and blood, and then despotism will not only be certain, it will even be desirable, as a relief from the harms of discord and civil war. This is no fancy sketch. It is the history of Rome, and to some extent of France. What will keep us from following in the same path, I may have occasion to notice before I close.

We see, then, that the republican form of government is not in all cases desirable. Our own government has recognized this principle. The inhabitants of the territory of Louisiana, at the time of its cession to the United States, were found to be so utterly incapable of self-government, that the legislative authority was vested in a council of thirteen, appointed annually by the President, from among the inhabitants of the territory.

In a community like the fabled republic of Plato, or the Utopia of Sir Thomas More, where all the inhabitants were endowed with unlimited intelligence and complete self-control; where they all knew what should be done, and were all willing to do it; nothing but a republic would be allowable, or indeed possible. And in a community of limited intelligence, and defective goodness, if they are not sunk too low, we will all agree that the republican form is the best for their present happiness and prosperity, and for their elevation and development. But if even into Utopia itself there should come a being far more wise and powerful, and of such superior goodness that all could confide in him, ought they not to make him govern? How much more should such blind and erring mortals, as we will all confess ourselves to be? Do we not act upon this principle every day? We confide our highest and most important interests to those who give, as we think, evidence of superior fitness for such guardianship.

After all our flourishes about the voice of the people being the voice of God, and "the sober second thoughts of the people," most of us follow the lead of some master-mind; thus endorsing the saying of a brilliant writer of our day, that "the true king or able man has a divine right to govern." But no mere man has a right, or should be allowed, to rule absolutely. Having but a limited intelligence, even if greatly superior to all his fellow men, he does not, and cannot, always know what course should be pursued. He needs to be aided and corrected by his fellow men; and an unwillingness to be thus advised, would be an indication of another tendency in human nature, which is by far the strongest objection to the possession of uncontrolled authority by man. Power is apt to corrupt its possessor—to make him selfish and ambitious, regardless of the wishes and wants of others. And if it does not do this, it begets in him an overweening self-confidence, which is as fatal to his subjects as deliberate wickedness.

> "Man, proud man,
> Dressed in a little brief authority,
> Most ignorant of what he 's most assured,
> His glossy essence,—like an angry ape,
> Plays such fantastic tricks before high heaven,
> As make the angels weep."

I would not trust the wisest and purest man that ever lived, with unlimited authority. There would always be some one among his inferiors, who could teach him in regard to some matters; and I should greatly fear that his head would be turned by such a giddy elevation.

But suppose there came among us some tall archangel, excelling in strength, his wisdom far transcending ours, his goodness unimpeachable, his power of resisting temptation sufficient for any emergency. Would it not be wise in us to give ourselves up to his guidance, implicitly—I had almost said, or at least to content ourselves with but a qualified veto on his actions? Still it might be possible that some of his measures would be unfortunate. We might learn to suspect his wisdom, even if we did not doubt his goodness. Having tasted the blessedness of such heavenly rule, would we not long to find some one of infinite, that is to say, unlimited wisdom, and irresistible power, whose goodness was equal to his intelligence and strength? Surely, we could confide implicitly in such a being. We should know that all his plans would be successful: that all his commands were for our good. If we found such a being, would it not be wise in us to enthrone him supreme monarch? Need I ask, where can such a being be found? Our Father in Heaven completely fills up, nay, if I may so speak, overflows the outline I have sketched. "Infinite, eternal, unchangeable, in his being, wisdom, power, holiness, justice, goodness and truth." Why should we not all pray, "Thy kingdom come?"

But let us examine the matter a little more closely. The laws of a people are generally considered a test of the character of the Sovereign. Look at the ten commandments, and for the purposes of this argument, I confine myself to the second table, regulating our intercourse with each other. Here we have all the principles of justice clearly and briefly enumerated. I do not wonder that the infidel lawyer, who began to read the Bible through, stopped here, crying out in astonishment, "Where did Moses get that law?" How came the leader of such a rude, barbarous horde, for such the Israelites must have been, and doubtless were, after centuries of bondage; how came their leader to announce with such terse simplicity, the great fundamental principles, upon which the legislation of all civilized nations is based? We do not estimate aright the greatness of this miracle, for a miracle it was, requiring the Divine interposition, in the form which we call inspiration; we do not estimate it properly, because we do not know, or remember, the real condition of the Israelites at the time of the Exodus. We fancy them such a people as we were at the Revolution. And Moses such a man as Washington, or Hamilton, or Jefferson. But they were slaves, and had been for ages, degraded and corrupted, as only oppression can degrade and corrupt. What should we think, if even now, the slaves of the South should march out, proclaiming and submitting to such an impartial code. True, the Israelites were in remote, and but remote contact, it must be remembered, with the highest civilization then existing; but it was an idolatrous civilization: how inferior to that to which our servile population is related. It cannot be denied that Moses was learned in all the wisdom of the Egyptians, but what was their knowledge compared with ours? And especially from it and the corrupt, despotic government, of which it was the support, how could he learn of the rights and duties of man? But in our fathers' veins flowed Anglo-Saxon blood. Hampden and St. Johns, Sidney and Russel, were their ancestors. Chatham and Burke were their cotemporaries. Is it strange that the constitution formed by the pupils of such men should be just and impartial? What if the slaves of the King of Dahomey should rise and promulgate sueh a code as the ten commandments? Yet even they might have caught some stray beams from the resplendent brightness of modern civilization. But in the case of Moses, we have the first, the earliest promulgation of the great fundamental principles of all jurisprudence. At the time when "God spake all these words," the darkness of barbarism was upon the face of the whole earth. Moses lived four hundred years before Homer, five hundred before Lycurgus, the founder of Sparta, and one thousand before Plato. And the succeeding ages of antiquity, so far from improving on him, have nothing that can compare with these brief but weighty commands. Compared with these, how cruel and blood-thirsty, how narrow and paltry, the code of Draco or the Decemviri, the institutions of Cadmus or Romulus. But they are not only the earliest, they are also the clearest enunciation of the great principles of justice the world has ever had. Every lawyer, however scanty his reading, may know that the jurisprudence of every civilized nation under heaven, whether it be of common or civil law, is based upon them. Any open, serious violation of them, "Speaking after the manner of men," would be adjudged a crime in every court in Christendom. How came, we may well ask, this leader of a barbarous people, this foster-child of a despot, to point out so plainly those eternal principles of justice, which should regulate the intercourse of men? Ah! it was God who spake all these words. This much, by way of episode, as to the divine authority and lofty grandeur of the Decalogue.

Would it not be a happy thing, if this could be the code of all nations? If all mankind

> Whether those
> Whom the sun's hot light darkens, or ourselves
> Whom he treats falsely, or the northern tribes,
> Whom ceaseless snows and starry winters bleach,

if all would settle down upon these principles of eternal justice, as the basis of their laws and usages, might we not hope for peace, peace like a river, and righteousness like the waves of the sea? And is not the coming of such a blessed era worth praying for? But there is much in the jurisprudence and legislation of even civilized and Christian nations, that conflicts with these commands of God. If any admiring disciple of Blackstone or Tribonian is inclined to doubt this, let us submit the matter to a simple test. The second table of the law is summed up and comprehended in the second great commandment. "Thou shalt love thy neighbor as thyself." Are there not many laws on the statute books of this nation, claiming to be, and perhaps rightfully, the most enlightened on the globe; to have the purest and most equitable code; are there not many laws permitting or authorizing a course of conduct directly contrary to this command? Let the kingdom of God fully come, let him be recognized as Sovereign, and his law as universally binding, and every vestige of such enactments would be swept away. Wrong doing and trickery, instead of being connived at, or protected by the law, as it is often complained that they are, would be frowned upon and rebuked. Ought we not to pray for the coming of the time when all our laws shall be framed and executed in the spirit of the rule so well called golden: "Whatsoever ye would that others should do unto you, do ye even so to them?"

But human legislation, even when purest and wisest, is but a weak endeavor after the sanctity of the divine law. There are many violations of our rights, there are many failures in duty, which positive enactment cannot reach. How much petty lying, for instance, and slander, which human law could never punish, but it is here all forbidden: "Thou shalt not bear false witness." The same may be said of the command, "Thou shalt not steal," and others. There are multitudes of men whose highest standard of morality is, the law of the land. If they are as good as that compels them to be, taking no more than it allows, and doing what it permits, they think themselves good enough. What progress should we witness in peace and morality, if all these persons could be brought to recognize the law of God as the rule to which they should conform, being a law unto themselves.

One great element of the power of the law over men, is the certainty of its execution. It is better to have a mild code, and strictly enforce it, than to stern and vigorous enactments, but suffer them have to be evaded and treated with contempt. But it is impossible to frame human laws so as to prevent evasion. Iniquity can almost always find some crevice through which to creep;

> "But it is not so above.
> There is no shuffling there; the action lies
> In its true nature, and we ourselves, compelled
> Even to the teeth and forehead of our faults,
> To give in evidence."

It will not be so here, when the kingdom of God shall come, and his law be recognized as the rule of conduct.

Human laws often operate unequally. They bear hard upon the innocent and the well-intentioned. It is impossible to frame them in such a way that they cannot be perverted by designing men for unjust purposes. The law of God can never be thus made the instrument of oppression. It is true and righteous altogether. The infinite wisdom and goodness of God will always secure the just and equal operation of his laws. I ask again, if the enthronement of such a being as absolute Sovereign, is not an event to be desired and prayed for?

So far, I presume, I shall carry every one with me. It must seem desirable that all men should regulate their intercourse with each other by the great principles of justice, laid down in the latter part of the ten commandments, and summed up in the second great commandment: "Thou shalt love thy neighbor as thyself." But there is a portion of the law of God, a first and great commandment, which regards our relations to our Father in Heaven. There are many persons, perhaps there are some such here, who, while they feel anxious that men should keep the second, care little if at all whether they obey the first. Or, in other words, while they are anxious that all should be moral, they have little desire that any should be religious. They regard Churches and Sabbath Schools only as they promote morality. If a sect or denomination only requires and enforces morality, no matter what false and dangerous ideas of God and our duty to him it may inculcate, it is good enough, and pure enough for them. They prize as highly, if not more so, him who is moral without being religious, than him who is moral because he is religious. It can hardly be expected of these persons, that they should pray, "Thy kingdom come," with an eye to such commands as, "Thou shalt love the Lord thy God with all thy heart:" or, "Thou shalt not take the name of the Lord thy God in vain." Yet, I think it can be shown, even on their own theory, that they ought to. I do not now address myself to my fellow Christians. We believe that the chief end of man is to glorify God, and to enjoy him forever. We hold that morality, as compared with religion, is but

——— "The silken tassel's flaunt,
Beside the golden corn."

But I wish to show the mere moralist that he ought to be as anxious that men should love God and reverence him, as that they should be honest and industrious. For obedience to the first commandment is the strongest possible guarantee of obedience to the second. If a man is truly religions, he must be moral; "every duty to man becoming doubly sacred as due also to God." And remember that in offering up this petition, you do not ask that men may make a profession of religion, but that they may *be* religious. The word of God everywhere teaches that this involves morality. "He who loveth not his brother, whom he hath seen, how can he love God whom he hath not seen." "See that none render evil for evil unto any man, but ever follow that which is good, both among yourselves and to all men. But again, religion is not only the surest, it is the only sure foundation for general morality. The religious feelings of man, his love to God, his reverence for God's law, his dread of God's displeasure, are the only holding ground in which his soul can anchor amid the storms of temptation that beset him. The great truth has been recognized by the most profound jurists, the most capable administrators of government. Mr. Webster, in his address at Plymouth, used the following language: "Our ancestors established their system of government on morality and religious sentiment. Moral habits, they believed, cannot safely be trusted on any other foundation than religious principle. Whatever makes men good Christians, makes them good citizens; and at the end of two centuries, there is nothing upon which we can pronounce more confidentially; nothing of which we can express a more deep and earnest conviction, than of the deep and inestimable importance of that religion to man, both in regard to this life and that which is to come." And again, in his Speech on the Girard Will Case, he says: "What would be the condition of our families, if religious fathers, and religious mothers were to teach their sons and daughters no religions tenets till they were eighteen? What would become of their morals, their character, their purity of heart and life? What would become of all that now renders the social circle lovely and beloved? What would become of society itself? How could it exist."

Washington, in his Farewell Address, teaches us that same lesson: "Of all the dispositions and habits which lead to political prosperity," he says, "religion and morality are indispensable supports. In vain would that man claim the tribute of patriotism who should labor to subvert these great pillars of happiness, these firmest props of the duties of men and citizens. The mere politician, equally with the pious man, ought to respect and cherish them. And let us with caution indulge the supposition that morality can be maintained without religion. Whatever may be conceded to the influence of refined education, or minds of peculiar structure, reason and experience both forbid us to expect that national morality can prevail in exclusion of religions principles."

This same truth is recognized also by our nation as a nation, both in the state and general governments. The halls of legislation are silent, the public offices are closed, the courts of law are deserted; and this great confederacy, in form at least, remembers the Sabbath day, to keep it holy. Nay, the laws of this state, and of almost every other state in the union, punish Sabbath-breaking and profanity as offences against the peace of society. And they do this, not on the ground that in committing these transgressions you invade the quiet of others, for you need not, and often would not, do this; but because whatever weakens the force of religious obligations, saps the very foundation of public order. True, these laws are seldom, if ever, enforced; nay, they are neglected and despised by the men who have made them, or have solemnly sworn to observe and execute them. But they stand, and long may they stand, the profane, Sabbath-breaking legislator's and judge's solemn condemnation of his own evil course. They show that the first table of the law is recognized in the basis of the second. True, it is only observance of the Sabbath, and reverence for God which are formally re-enacted. Yet this secures the principles. And I am of the opinion that the worship of a strange God, or the idolatrous worship of the one living and true God, would be equally at war with the spirit of our legislation, founded as that is upon the common law of England. Of one thing there can be no doubt. The laws of the land protect and encourage religion. Infidelity is tolerated. *Atheism* is tolerated. And let them be. Heathenism would be tolerated. I am not sure but it is in California now. But religion, and the Christian religion, alone is sanctioned and cherished.

Here, then, you see that wise and enlightened legislators have always put a high estimate upon religious motives and obligations. Would you be wiser than they? Would you be indifferent to that of which they were so solicitous? And let me tell you, worldly-minded, scheming, money-making, money-loving man, it is of great importance to you, that the religion which controls the community, should be the purest possible. The more correct its teachings as to what man is to believe concerning God, and what duty God requires of man, the more efficacious will it be in preserving the morality, and thus securing the welfare of society. Would you be prosperous and happy? Would you have all men share in that prosperity? Lift up, then, your heart to our Father in Heaven, and say, "Thy kingdom come."

Of all people in the world, the citizens of a republic should offer this petition most earnestly. While religion is a great support and preservative of any government, it is absolutely essential to the bare existence of one that assumes a democratic form. We could not live in a republic where there was not some reverence for God and his laws. In the eloquent language of the instructor of my youth,—"While a democracy in which every man should love God, and his neighbor, as himself, would be well,"—nay, I hold it the best possible on earth,—"an infidel and atheistic democracy, manifesting, as it certainly would, the animalism of the brute with the art and malignity of the fiend, would give us the most vivid image of hell upon earth of which we can conceive." There is, I fear,—and sometimes among Christian men too,—"a kind of worship of democracy," a fluent dogmatism about free institutions and manifest destiny; as if there was something in our mere form of government to preserve and perpetuate it. But a republic of Sabbath-breakers and debauchees cannot prosper, Anglo Saxon though they be. It is not our war-steamers on the high seas, our foot and artillery on the frontiers, the eloquent orator, or the shrewd politician, that are the defence and protection of our land. No: the humble, pious mother, the faithful minister of the Gospel, these are the bulwarks of our freedom.

Other men may look to other sources of strength, to the diffusion of knowledge, the multiplication of useful inventions, the increase of wealth and refinements, but to me there is no hope for us, but in the coming of the kingdom of God. Schools and colleges may rise in every quarter; learned and laborious Professors may be there; crowds of eager students may throng around them. We may have all knowledge, and understand all mysteries in heaven and earth; our barns and out-houses may be bursting with fullness; railroads and telegraph-wires may cover the land like a net-work; but if religion loses its hold upon us; if we cast off fear and restrain prayer before God, our wealth and knowledge will only furnish us more abundant means of profligacy. Our government, our nation, will be rotten to the very core, and anarchy, with its sure successor, despotism, will stand at the door. Fellow-citizen, whom I may not call fellow-Christian, would you save our common country from this awful doom? Pray, then, with us, "Thy kingdom come." Help us to bring in that kingdom. Help us to send into every hamlet and habitation the Bible, the Sabbath-School, and the preacher; mighty through God to the pulling down of the strong holds of sin.

Are you a propagandist, anxious that free institutions should absorb the Continent, sweep over Europe, and encircle the globe? Then, even you, too, must pray, "Thy kingdom come." I have already shown that a republican government is, in its last analysis, literal self-government. Even the few, and they are very few, who are naturally capable, to some extent, of this self-government, will be greatly assisted by "the grace of God that bringeth salvation. "When a man is trained up to become a subject of the kingdom of heaven, he will be best fitted to be a good citizen in a free government." But, with the mass of men, as has been already remarked, there is no security. There is no basis for this self-government, so essential to free institutions, but the religion of the Bible. If, then, you would break every yoke, and let the oppressed go free, you must send this religion, with its influences and institutions, to every part of the world.—Nothing but the coming of the kingdom of God can destroy all earthly kingdoms, and this certainly will. Let Christianity thoroughly pervade all ranks and classes, and tyranny would be impossible. Then all in authority would feel that they were representatives, not substitutes for nations, and

"——That to rule in slavery and error,
For the mere ends of personal pomp and power,
Is such a sin as doth deserve a hell
To its self sole."

And a nation of godly men could not be enslaved. They would call no man master, for one is their master, even Christ. The Son would make them free, and they would be free indeed, with the liberty of the sons of God. And if not thus made free, they must be slaves, the slaves of low desires; "slaves to a horde of petty tyrants," military chieftains, demagogues, time-serving politicians, political soldiery of fortune, "stating, with ordinary oaths, their love to every new position." Nations should learn, and they are learning, that

> "It is not kings
> Nor priests they need fear, so much as themselves;
> That if they keep but true to themselves, and pure,
> Sober, enlightened, godly—mortal men
> Become impassable as air, one great
> And indestructible substance as the sea."

I do not say that, wherever Christianity prevails, it will immediately or necessarily produce revolution, and dethrone monarchs. The process will be gradual, and it is best that it should. The forms of royalty may to some extent remain, long after the people really exercise the sovereign power. The passage to entire self-government, in form as well as in fact, may be peaceful, and perhaps even imperceptible. But when the hour comes for that change, the people will be ready for it, and eventually it will come. This is illustrated in the case of the Sandwich Islands. For a long time, the king has had but nominal power, and now they, who, thirty years ago, were the barbarous slaves of a cruel despot, as barbarous as themselves, are asking admittance into our confederacy. Who has done this? Philosophers and orators, theorizing and declaiming about popular sovereignty? No, indeed: a handful of ministers of the cross, whom orators and philosophers have been laughing to scorn. Lo! "what hath God wrought!"

The same process is going on in Great Britain. True, they have a queen, but she rides in her carriage amid admiring and applauding thousands, to open Parliament, with as little real power over the destinies of England and of Europe, as the boy prince at her side, the heir apparent to the throne. The people govern. Public opinion is heard and respected. No administration could stand there twenty-four hours against the opposition of the nation. It cannot be denied that there are great abuses there, and glaring inequalities, but they are constantly attacked by many sober, enlightened, godly men. They are being alleviated, and I hope and believe will be ultimately removed, till at last no traces shall remain, of oppressive and arbitrary distinctions in society. Every humane man, indeed, every man who is not dyed in red republicanism, must wish that this change might come by the voluntary renunciation and sacrifice of the royal family and nobility. Who could wish to see anarchy and civil war running riot over that fair land,

"Refinement's chosen seat,
Art's trophied dwelling, learning's green retreat?"

Who would not rather see king, queen and lords, driven by no dire necessity, but led by their love to God and their fellow-men, willingly resigning their place and power. I am not without hope that Christianity will yet present us with this grand spectacle. But if this change must come, as the consequence of a revolution, and I think in some form or other it will come, the crisis will be comparatively brief and peaceful. There will at least be no reign of terror, nothing of that wild intoxication, that blood-thirsty anarchy, which disgraced France. They are better fitted now for free institutions than any nation on the globe, except our own; and when the preper time comes, they will take their place among the republics of the world, with the calmness and firmness of Christian men. And as the kingdom of God comes, as Christianity finds its way deeper and deeper into the hearts of men, the process will go on. Fetter after fetter will be broken, slave after slave will join the anthem of the free,

"Till nation after nation, taught the strain,
Earth rolls the rapturous hosannah round."

If, then, you love liberty and your fellow-men, though you are a republican, though you are a radical, you must pray, "Thy kingdom come," that princes and prelates and popes may be nothing, and God almighty may be all in all.

My Christian friends, what infinite motives urge us to pray this prayer, earnestly and unceasingly. While the great majority of our fellow-men are sending after Christ, the Immanuel, God with us, and saying "We will not have this man to reign over us;" we are his subjects, his soldiers, looking for and hasting unto the coming of God, our Savior. To advance the interests, and to secure the triumph of his kingdom, we are united together as a Church. For this purpose you have built this house; for this purpose I stand here Sabbath after Sabbath; to this purpose I have devoted my life. To accomplish it, you spend cheerfully, and indeed gladly, as I hope and believe, your time and money; nay, more—you labor in your worldly business, in your stores and your shops, cheerfully, that you may do something for him who does so much for you. To hasten the coming of the kingdom, we labor in the reforms of the day. Other men may aim at other ends; the increase of physical comfort and social well-being; but the mark of the prize of our high calling, is the coming of the kingdom of God. Any religion that makes men industrious, intelligent and peaceful, may satisfy the philanthropist and the republican, but nothing can fill the compass of our hopes and prayers, but the coming of the Son of man, "a second time, without sin, unto salvation." Why should we not pray for the realization of our fondest wishes?

"Oh that the Son
Might come again. There should be no more war,
No more want; no more sickness; with a touch
He shall cure all diseases, and with a word all sin."

There is yet another reason why we should pray, "Thy kingdom come." Every pious heart must feel oppressed with a painful consciousness that the kingdom of God has not yet come. It has not yet fully come in our hearts. We are often rebellious, and always forgetful subjects; and the world lieth in wickedness, or, as it might be translated, under the power of the evil one. The prince of the power of the air rules the nations. Even in Christian lands, what pride and oppression, what malignity and deceit, what practical atheism; and oh! how full are the dark places of the earth of the habitations of cruelty. Who can overcome this opposition? None but God. We have this treasure in earthen vessels, that the excellency of the power may be of God, and not of man. Well, then, in our utter helplessness, may we cry to our Father in heaven, "Thy kingdom come;" and blessed be God, that kingdom shall come. The mountain of the house of the Lord shall be established in the top of the mountains, and it shall be exalted above the hills, and all nations shall flow unto it.

"The day shall yet appear,
When the might with the right and the truth shall be;
And come what there may, to stand in the way,
That day the world shall see."

Whether our nation, "heir of all the ages foremost in file of time," with such pre-eminent facilities and opportunities for forwarding this kingdom, shall aid in this great work, we cannot be sure. If she is false to her solemn trust, if bribery and deceit and oppression rule, if she is a Christian nation only in name, she is lost.—"Thou art weighed in the balances, and art found wanting," will be written on her walls, as truly as on those of tyrannous, luxurious Babylon of old. But if, as we hope and pray, she holds fast, and does not deny the name of Christ, every thing teaches us to believe she will have much to do in bringing in the latter-day glory. Then do we believe, to quote again the language of the Gamaliel at whose feet I was brought up, "there will be in our ship of state, as we believe there always has been, one who, though he may seem for a time to be asleep in the hinder part of the vessel, will yet come when the winds are loudest and the waves are highest, and say, 'Peace, be still.'"

But should we, which may God forbid, reject the counsel of God against ourselves, his kingdom will come. Whatever may become of our nation, yea, of our sect or party in the Church, the ark of God will ride triumphant over every billow. The kingdoms of this world shall become the kingdoms of our Lord and of his Christ.

Yes, my brother, however dark and discouraging the prospect may seem, relax none of your efforts, cease not your importunate prayers; nay, rather, double your diligence. The kingdom of God shall come. It may come quickly. This tempestuous state of things at present may be simply

> "The waking of a sea
> Before a calm, that rocks itself to rest."

Or it may be, as I am inclined to believe, that the wars and rumors of wars which disquiet the whole earth, are the foreshadowings of the great and final contest between truth and error, between God and the great enemy of God and man.—We may fall in the midst of the battle. The youngest disciple of Christ who hears me, may die amid the gloom and darkness of this apparently uncertain conflict; but he whose right it is, shall reign, and we, whether in the body or out of the body, shall swell with rapture that song of grateful homage: "We give thee thanks, Lord God almighty, that thou hast taken to thyself thy great power, and hast reigned."

SERMON IV.

Thy will be done in earth, as it is done in heaven.
Matt. 6: 10.

This petition is the complement, the counterpart of the preceding one. In the former we pray that God's kingdom may come; in the latter, that men may be obedient subjects of that kingdom. The one without the other would be invoking upon ourselves the direst possible curse; for if we should see clearly and constantly our obligation to obey God, and yet not obey him, how bitter must be our remorse. The reason why men live so contentedly in disobedience to their Heavenly Father, is that they are almost all insensible, while none are fully alive to his kingly authority; and one cause of this deadness is the fact that "judgment against an evil work is not executed speedily. Judgment for a long time lingereth, and damnation slumbereth." But, as was remarked in discussing that subject, page 59, when the kingdom of God shall come, there will be no more of the law's delay. Every transgression will promptly secure its due recompense and reward. Men will, on this, as well as on other accounts, be fully aware and unceasingly conscious of their allegiance to God, and there will therefore be an end, necessarily, of the pleasure of sin, which they now enjoy for a season.

This, I believe, will be the condition of the finally impenitent. All the ignorance and stupidity, the blindness and hardness of heart, which keep men at ease in their wickedness here, will be removed. Every bleared eye will be cleansed, every torpid conscience will be awakened. The glorious attributes of God will be revealed to them with overpowering distinctness, and the whole creation will have neither nook nor corner where they can hide themselves from this display of his majesty. They will feel their obligation to love and obey their Heavenly Father, not only as they do not now feel it, but with a force and strength of which they can now form no conception. Yet they will not love and serve him. They will see, with anguish and agony, the guilt of every sin, but will still persist in sin; as the drunkard, even here, feels the folly and shame of his bondage to appetite, yet will not, *cannot* break away. If, then, we would not have this hell upon earth, when we pray—"thy kingdom come," we must at the same time ask that the will of God may be done on earth as it is done in heaven.

The most obvious lesson to be derived from this petition is the duty of being contented with the allotments of Providence. Most Christians, in their use of this prayer, employ this petition in no other sense but as expressing their acquiescence in God's purposes respecting them. This is undoubtedly correct, so far as it goes. We do here submit our wills, even in our most importunate requests, to the will of God. The spirit of this petition should be in every prayer, though it is to be feared that this disposition is not so uniform an element of our prayers, especially when they are ardent and sincere, as it ought to be. Our desires after spiritual good are generally so faint and languid, that we are seldom troubled with fears and inquietude, lest the feeble, formal prayers we offer, should be disregarded. But when we come to ask for temporal blessings, or even think of our dependence on the providence of God for them, how apt we are to have a rebellious, or at least a repining or unquiet spirit. And sometimes, too, when our hearts are burdened with the thought of the multitudes around us, casting off fear and restraining prayer; or, when grieved and heart-broken at the sight of some dear friend, a husband, a wife, or a child, without God, and of course without hope in the world; in the bitterness of our souls we are tempted to complain of God; or, when hearing of powerful revivals elsewhere, while all is cold and dead among us; or, when seeing a fair prospect of growth in the Church suddenly blasted by some unpropitious circumstance, some sudden turn in the tide of events, do we not murmur that we alone are left desolate?

My brethren, we are always to cherish the spirit of this petition in our efforts, as well as in our prayers. In our labors and sufferings, we are always to say, "thy will be done;" and we are not to reserve this feeling for great occasions and severe trials. In the petty vocations of every day, in the constantly recurring routine of life's dull duties, this spirit may, and should be manifested. He who taught us this prayer, is himself our example in regard to this. In the hour of his extremest agony and peril, he said: "O, my Father, if this cup may not pass away from me except I drink it, thy will be done." The Lord grant that we may all be baptized with the same spirit.

That we pray in this petition for such a disposition, appears upon the surface; but a deeper and an equally important lesson is taught in it. Neither its spirit nor its literal meaning can be limited to mere passive endurance. It reaches and includes the active powers of our nature. You would hardly look to find what is commonly called Calvinism in the Lord's prayer; but here it is, in one of its most offensive forms, in this expression: "Thy will be done." This is not the language of acquiescence and submission merely, as in the case of our Savior, but of earnest entreaty, that it may be our meat and our drink, as it was his, to do the will of our Father in heaven. We confess our utter inability, as of ourselves, to do the will of God. Distrusting and disowning our own strength, we ask God to bring to pass the doing of his will by us. The Apostle Paul felt this. He says: "When I would do good, evil is present with me. Oh, wretched man that I am, who shall deliver me from the body of this death? I thank God, through our Lord Jesus Christ." And every converted soul has felt the same meekness, and has looked to the same source for strength. Even unconverted men feel and confess this inability, though they do not go to God for help. The great dramatist of our language, who gives portraitures of human nature inferior only to those of Holy Writ, and who cannot be suspected of any leaning to stern orthodoxy, puts this strong, but by no means exaggerated language into the mouth of a murderer, full of remorse:

"Try what repentance can; what can it not?
Yet, oh! what can it, when one can't repent?"

This inability to do what we know we should, and perhaps wish to do, is part of our sad heritage in our present estate of sin and misery. But in what does this inability consist? in what part of man's nature do we find the weakness, the defect which disables him? This is a question which demands patient and thoughtful consideration. May the Father of Lights grant us the guidance of his Holy Spirit, while we proceed to investigate it. The first and great, the fundamental command is, "Thou shalt love the Lord thy God with all thy heart." Now, man evidently has intellect necessary to understand this. He can know God; not that he can fully comprehend his nature, but he can know that there is a God, and be, to some extent, aware of his character. A brute or an idiot cannot do this. They are, therefore, incapable of doing the will of God. But man has, we see, intellectual ability. He is capable, also, of exercising the required affection—he can love. Now, it is possible to imagine a being of pure intellect, incapable of any affection. I do not, of course, suppose God ever created such a being; indeed, I doubt whether such a being could be created; but we can conceive of such an one. Now the command, "Thou shalt love the Lord thy God with all thy heart," addressed to such a being, would be a mockery. He could see and understand the character of God, but he could not feel any emotion resulting from such perceptions of God's attributes. But man can exercise this affection, and therefore he is in this sense able to do the will of God. Man has also a conscience, to which this command may be addressed. He can feel the force of moral obligation,—he can see, and to some extent he does see, that he ought to obey God. If he did not, or rather could not, he would be incapable of obedience. What, then, is the inability of man to do the will of God? It is his want of the dispositiou to do it. This last kind of ability is often called moral, while the others are called natural. Man is said, therefore, by those who use these terms, to have natural ability, but moral inability. It is generally believed, I think, that our Church does not adopt this distinction. It seems to me, any candid person will see that our standards teach the doctrine I have already advanced, that man's inability is his want of disposition. "Man, by his fall into a state of sin, hath wholly lost all ability of will to any spiritual good accompanying salvation."* The Larger Catechism, in answer to Question 25, describes the corruption of man's nature, as "that whereby he is indisposed, disabled, and made opposite to all good, and wholly inclined to evil."

But there are those who believe that our branch of the Church puts such a construction upon these passages—gives them such an interpretation—as to believe and teach that man has no ability of any kind to obey the law of God. This is a great

* Conf. Faith, Chap. 9, Sec. 3.

mistake. It would be easy to show that the view of inability I have taken is recognized as the orthodox one, by the most thorough Calvinists. I shall quote, at this time, only a few modern authors, to show what our belief really is.

Dr. Green, the nestor of our Church, quoted the following expression, as giving his views: "The moral inability under which sinners lie as a consequence from the fall, is not of such a nature as to take away the guilt of sin." The venerable Dr. Mathews, for many years a Professor in our Theological Seminary in this State, says: "We possess, indeed, all the natural facilities which God demands in his service, but we are without the moral power. We have not the disposition, the desire to employ them in his service." Dr. A. G. Fairchild, in his work entitled, "The Great Supper," published by our Board, uses the following language: "Sinners are urged to come to Christ, inasmuch as their inability is an inability of the will. The reason that they cannot truly come to the Savior is, that they are not cordially willing. It is not their choice to come. Their voluntary blindness, their love of sin and aversion to holiness, are what disable them. We do not therefore teach that sinners are bound hand and foot, and thus prevented from coming to Christ, though desirous of doing so. This is a palpable misrepresentation of our sentiments.

They would be able if they were truly willing." Could any thing be more explicit?

While we all accept the view I have given of the nature of man's inability, there are some in our branch of the Church, who believe—and I am one—that the terms, natural ability and moral inability, do not accurately describe the condition of man, and had therefore better not be employed. Our objections to them are as follows:

The language used conveys the idea that man's unwillingness to obey the will of God is not natural to him. Now we believe, as I have no doubt most of those who use the language I am condemning do, that it is; that is to say, it belongs to all men: it is a part of our nature. We bring it into the world with us. It is the very essence of that depravity, which we all agree to call native, or natural. Our inability, that is, our unwillingness, is not natural in precisely the same sense as our intellect, our affections and conscience. God did not endow us with it, but it is natural in an important sense: which the distinction between natural and moral, as commonly made, slights and overlooks.

Again, man's ability may be said to be moral. It is not a physical ability that we contend for, but a moral; an ability which is in the intellect, the affections, the conscience. These are the moral faculties in man. The possession of them makes man a moral, accountable being, a subject of moral government; that is, government by motives—by reason instead of force. So that man has a moral ability to do the will of God. This may seem to some captious quibbling, but it is not intended to be such. We, who object to the phases under consideration, are persuaded that it is of great importance that our language upon these points should be as precise and accurate as possible. While we agree with those who use these terms, as to the nature and seat of man's inability, we prefer to describe it as being in his will or disposition. We know of no better description of it than that already quoted, "man is indisposed, disabled, and made opposite to all spiritual good."

I have been sometimes inclined to suspect that our branch of the Church differs from others in regard to another aspect of this subject. We hold, as they do, that man's inability results from, or rather consists in, such a perversion of his nature as makes him opposed to spiritual good, and inclined to evil; but we hold, also, that this perversion of his nature has extended, in a measure, to his intellect and conscience; has infected and corrupted them, so that he does not see God's attributes—does not perceive their moral beauty, and feel his obligation to love God for them, as clearly and strongly as he would, if he had never become indisposed, disabled, and opposite to all spiritual good. Revelation seems to us to teach this doctrine. This is what we understand the Bible to mean, when it represents men as having "the understanding darkened, being alienated from the life of God through the ignorance that is in them, because of the blindness of their hearts; having their foolish heart darkened," and other parallel passages which I might quote. We think that reason would lead us to expect, that the corruption of man's affections would thus extend to his intellect and his conscience; and we believe—nay, we are sure, that the testimony of experience is on our side. Will not every Christian acknowledge that, in his unconverted state, he did not see such loveliness in the character of God—so much that ought to awaken his admiration—that he did not feel so strongly as he now does his obligation to love and serve God? And will he not confess that the reason why God's character is not more attractive to him now, and that he is not more sensible of his duty to love God is, the corruption remaining in him, which blinds his eyes and hardens his heart? What is this but to acknowledge that the perversion of his nature extends to his intellect and his conscience?

Now, it has sometimes appeared to me, that those who impute to us extreme and unreasonable views in regard to man's inability, do not look at this particular point as we do. But, on reviewing the matter, I am inclined to think that they have slighted this phase of the question. They have entirely mistaken our opinions. Supposing that we hold that man has no kind of ability, in any degree, to do the will of God, in their zeal to vindicate God and man from such an aspersion, for such it is, in their well-meant endeavors to prove to us what we have never denied, that man has enough of what they call natural ability, to make him responsible, they forget to acknowledge, what I cannot think they would deny, that the corruption of man's nature has impaired his faculties. I would remark here, in passing, that much of the harsh language of the old writers is to be understood as asserting, that man's reason and conscience have been weakened, as a consequence of the fall. When this is remembered, it gives a very different meaning to many of their expressions, which, taken alone, and out of their connection, seem to deny man the possession of any ability whatever to do the will of God.

I have seen it asserted, lately, by high authority, that the difference between us and those who hold a looser theology is, that while we agree as to the nature of man's inability, they look upon it as under man's control, and we do not. They say, he has only to determine to love God, and he can do it. We believe that, however much he may resolve and re-resolve, he will never do the will of God, until God works in him, both to will and to do. If this is the difference between us, it is certainly of no small importance. I must confess I have seen the former of these views avowed in some influential quarters; but I cannot believe that the majority of those who suppose us to hold illiberal and absurd opinions in regard to man's inability, attribute to him such a control over his own evil disposition. The teachings of the Bible are plainly to the contrary. "No man," said our Savior himself, "can come unto me, except the Father draw him." And shortly afterwards he repeats the same saying: "No man can come unto me, except it were given him of my Father." And, yet again, he tells his disciples in his parting instructions, "without me ye can do nothing." "Not that we are sufficient of ourselves," says the Apostle, "to think any thing as of ourselves." "Can the Ethiopian change his skin," said God by the mouth of the prophet, "or the leopard his spots? Then may ye also do good who are accustomed to do evil." Those who become the sons of God, are represented as being born, not of the will of man, but of God. The language of our Confession of Faith is equally explicit. Not that I would put this upon a level with the Word of God, but I introduce its declarations here, to show how they coincide with the teachings of Holy Writ; and also to convince you that no one can subscribe to that venerable instrument, without rejecting the idea that man can turn to God whenever he pleases. "Man, by his fall into a state of sin and misery," say the Westminster Assembly of Divines, "hath wholly lost all ability of will to any spiritual good accompanying salvation; so as a natural man, being wholly averse from that which is good, and dead in sin, is not able by his own strength to convert himself, or prepare himself thereto."

This is the experience of every Christian. "I know too much," said a warm-hearted Methodist brother to me, in speaking of one who had preached, as he said, the doctrine that it was as easy for a sinner to turn round and be a Christian, as for him to take a right-hand or a left-hand road that happened to lead where he wished to go; "I know too much," said this devout man, "of the agony of a sinner under conviction, ever to believe that." And do we not all know too much of our own utter helplessness, to believe that man can convert himself, or prepare himself thereto? The experience of the awakened soul is of the same character. "My nature," said such an one to a minister of the Gospel, "is stronger than my will." Ah, how true! The passionate man, shedding bitter tears over his haste and injustice—the drunkard, reeling home to that disgraced family, before whom and his God he has so often sworn to abstain forever,—indeed, all kinds and classes of men must make the same sad confession. At least, I cannot think it possible, that any intelligent person, professing to believe what is commonly called Calvinism, in its most liberal phases, can believe that man's evil propensities are under the control of his will.

There are two classes of objectors to the sentiments I have advanced, both, perhaps, represented here. Some of you will say, "I do not believe any such doctrine. Man has full power to do the will of God; he can repent, reform, change his course of conduct, obey God, whenever he pleases." Well, my friend, do it: make the experiment.

You do not love to read the Bible, to pray, to associate with Christians. You do not love God with all your heart, and your neighbor as yourself. Resolve, now, that you will do all this; that you will perform, faithfully, all the duties God's word enjoins, and what success will you have? You are the people that say, if you ever make a profession of religion, you will show Church-members how to live. Ah, you do not know the force of your own evil tendencies. Because you are floating down the stream, you think there is no current; but turn and breast it, and you will soon see with what irresistible power, (irresistible by your own strength,) it sweeps you along. I say again, make the experiment. Many an awakened sinner has made it before you, and has discovered his own weakness, nay, utter inability to do the will of God. The Lord grant that you may find this out before it is too late, and may flee for refuge to the hope set before you in the Gospel.

But some one will say, on the other hand, "I believe this: I have an evil heart: I cannot change it: God only can. He will do so, if he sees fit, and I must wait till he does see proper to do so." Now, of you who make this profession, one of two things is true. Either you do not think it such a bad thing to be unwilling to obey God, or you do not truly believe that God alone can remove this unwillingness.

If you felt yourself to be dangerously sick, and were persuaded that none but the most skillful physician could save you, how eagerly would you search for—how earnestly would you beseech such an one.

But if you think yourself only a little, or not at all unwell, or believe that, however sick you may be, you are fully capable of managing your disease, you will have no anxiety for assistance. So, too, if you felt the wretchedness and guilt of sin; if you were really persuaded that no one but

God could deliver you from that body of death, with what passionate importunity, what groans and sighs, would you cry to him for help. I know you do not feel the danger and the woe of your present condition; you do not think yourself, as the Apostle did, a wretched man, because you do not love and obey God; because there is a law of sin and death in your members. I long to see you feeling this, this conviction of sin, which shall drive you to God as your only resource. And if you would investigate the matter, I think you would find that you are not relying so entirely on the help of God. You think, after all, that, by and by, when you get ready, you can of yourself repent; that is, change your heart and your affections. Oh, that I could really convince you that this is not so; that I could make you feel your utter inability, of your own strength, to convert yourself. I should look to see you finding your way to God by Him who has said, "Whosoever cometh unto me, I will in no wise cast out."

There are some who will say, All this may be true; but we do not think it is best to preach it, it does more harm than good. I reply, that when we say the sinner cannot of himself come to Christ, and do the will of God, we say only what Christ and his Apostles said; and we are not afraid to follow their guidance.

Besides, if the sinner cannot of himself turn to

God, he ought to know it. If you tell him that he can, or lead him to suppose that he can, he will be completely at ease, and will wait till he is ready, instead of seizing the appointed time, and the day of salvation. In not plainly showing him his helpless condition, you flatter him into a false and dangerous peace.

There is yet another class of persons, to whom I must address myself. Sometimes you find professors of religion among them, though I hope no member of this Church has any such feeling. Generally, these persons are moral men, and what are commonly called, moralists; a class to whom may be applied the preface to the parable of the Publican and the Pharisee: "They trust in themselves that they are righteous, and despise others." What do these people say? "What is the use of all this dull, doctrinal preaching; what has it to do with your text? Give us a plain, practical sermon." My friends, we are told in our form of government, that "truth is in order to goodness;" and this is sound philosophy. You cannot have correct practice, without sound doctrine. What would you think of a student in medicine, who should say to his instructor, "What is the use of all this study about the theory of medicine? let us practice." Would you want such an one to practice on you?

The truth I have been endeavoring to unfold

is eminently a practical one, and appropriate to our present subject. You will never pray this prayer as you should, "Thy will be done," till you feel your utter inability, of yourself, to do the will of God. If you are a professor of religion, you will not pray so earnestly, nor so often as you should, for grace to help in every time of need, until you are convinced that you can of your own self do nothing; that, as the branch cannot bear fruit of itself, except it abide in the vine, no more can you, except you abide in Christ. My impenitent friend, you will never ask God for mercy—you will never cry, "Lord, save or I perish," until you feel that unless he does save, you will perish. You see, then, how important it is that this conviction of your utter helplessness should be waked up in your heart. The Lord grant that we may all so feel our dependence upon him, that we shall send up together this importunate prayer, "Thy will be done."

Perhaps you are one of those who say you would join the Church, you would make a profession of religion, you would begin a Christian life, if you only thought you could carry it out. For *you*, this subject has a deep significance. You need first of all to learn, that you cannot of yourself carry it out, nor begin it, and that you must ask God to help you. Your language will then be, "thanks be to God, who *giveth us* the victory, through our Lord Jesus Christ."

But we pray that the will of God may be done in a certain manner—"as it is done in heaven." No better explanation of this comprehensive phrase can be given, than that which was drawn out by a Sabbath School teacher, in his examination of his class. However familiar any of us may be with this simple story, it will do us good to be reminded, that while God hides these things from the wise and prudent, he reveals them unto babes. "You have told me, my children," said a teacher, "where the will of God is to be done, on earth, and how it is to be done, as it is done in heaven. How do you think the angels, and the happy spirits, do the will of God in heaven, as they are to be our pattern?" The first child replied, "they do it immediately." The second, "they do it diligently." The third, "they do it always." The fourth, "they do it with all the heart." The fifth, "they do it altogether.

Here a pause ensued, and no child appeared to have an answer ready. But after some time a little girl arose and said, "why, sir, they do it without asking any questions." How suggestive is every one of these replies. Let us do the will of God immediately, never deferring it to a more convenient season. Let us do it diligently, not with listless indolence. Some professors of religion are very active and enterprising in their worldly affairs, but slow and careless in everything that pertains to the glory of God, and the good of their souls. They do not do the will of God as it is done in heaven. Let us do it always; not simply when we shall gain influence, or friends, or money by it. Not when we have no temptation to do otherwise; not simply when we are among Christians, or in times of religious excitement; but at all times, in all places, under all circumstances.

Let us do it with all our hearts; not reluctantly, not driven to it by fear, but because we love to do it. Whoever of us shall thus do the will of God, shall have the peace of God that passeth knowledge.

"He that hath light in his own clear heart,
May sit in the centre and enjoy bright day."

But if this little company, who are banded together as members of the Church of Christ, could do the will of God altogether, no jarring, no contention, no suspicion, what bliss would be ours. Like the multitude of them that believed after the pentecostal visitation of the Spirit, we should be of one heart and soul.

And if to all this we could add such sweet submission, such confidence, that He doeth all things well, as to do the will of God without asking any questions, never doubting, never fearful, never curious, what a daguerreotype of heaven the sun-light of love would paint, even on the sin-darkened face of earth. Who will not pray, "Thy will be done on earth, as in heaven." I cannot help thinking that this prayer will be granted. I have not yet thoroughly investigated the subject, but my childhood faith still clings fondly to that grand old theory of a personal reign of Christ upon the earth.

"Through the harsh noises of our day,
A low, sweet prelude finds its way;
Through clouds of doubt, and creeds of fear,
A light is breaking, calm and clear.

"That song of Love—now low and far,
Ere long shall swell from star to star;
That light, the breaking day, which tips
The golden-spired apocalypse."

SERMON V.

Give us this day our daily bread.—Matt. 6 : 11.

The position of this, in relation to the other petitions of the Lord's Prayer, is somewhat remarkable. We make general request for the hallowing of God's name, for the coming of his kingdom, and the doing of his will as it is done in heaven, before we ask anything for ourselves individually. Little as this may arrest the attention of the casual reader, or even repeater of the prayer, it has a deep significance. This subordination of our own needs to the glory of God, and the welfare of man, this forgetting of our own individual necessities in a sense of the wants and woes of a sinful world, is an essential element of the true spirit of prayer. Worldly-minded men sometimes say, they do not believe in the efficacy of prayer, for they have tried it, and it did no good. A man once told me, that he had prayed every Sunday morning for a year, and was none the better for it. Might not such persons find an explanation of this anomaly in the fact, that they have never had that supreme and absorbing regard for the glory of God, which is essential to true prayer? "Ye ask and receive not," says the apostle James, "because ye ask amiss;" and then he goes on to explain what he means by asking amiss, "that ye may consume it upon your lusts." Men ask for their own personal gratification, for health for instance, but not that they may have strength to labor for the glory of God; for wealth, but not that they may spend it in God's service, and for the good of their fellow men. They ask these things of God because they feel their dependence upon him for them. But this consciousness of dependence gives them no pleasure; they do not love to think how completely God overrules their plans, and how he sometimes thwarts them.

They would gladly be independent of him, if they could be. How different is this from the, "Thy will be done," which should always precede every request for temporal good.

And even when such an one prays for "the forgiveness of sin, and the life everlasting," it is from a selfish fear of punishment, or a desire to be happy. Of course these may be, and I think always are, among the motives which lead men to trust in Christ, and properly so it is. But they are not to be the sole or supreme motives. They are such, however, with a worldly-minded, irreligions man, when he asks for "the blessings Jesus has to give." What cares he for the glory of

God, and the honor of his law, if he himself may be safe? And when, as in the case of the moralist, he thinks he can save himself; or, as in the case of the Universalist, he has persuaded himself that in his present irreligious condition, he is safe, it is little he troubles himself to pray to God, to praise him, to read his word. I do not mean to say that there are none who believe in the salvation of all men, who are devout lovers of the service of God. I have no doubt there are such; it has been my privilege to be acquainted with some: but they form a meagre minority of those who hold the doctrine in question. Generally, the louder a man is, in his assertions of this belief, and the more confident he seems to become of his own safety, the less and less does he care for God, and the Bible, and prayer.

But there are those who are as confident of their safety as these persons can be, who

"Can read their titles clear,
To mansions in the skies;"

having attained to what the apostle calls the full assurance of hope. This does not make *them* indifferent to the service of God. Nay, the more confident they become, the more devout are they in fearing and worshiping our Father in Heaven.

"If any man be a worshiper of God, and

doeth his will," we are told in the Holy Scriptures, "him he heareth." Now the men who say they have prayed, and it did no good, are not worshipers of God, but of themselves; their supreme affection is for themselves. They cannot ask, as the first and chief desire of their hearts, "hallowed be thy name." They do not hallow it; nay, some of them at times blaspheme that worthy name. Neither can they pray with the heart, "thy kingdom come." They may have no particular objections to the setting up of that kingdom, but they do not long for it. What they desire is, individual good, and personal safety, no matter what becomes of the cause of the King of kings. And indeed, they are not willing that the kingdom of God should come in their own hearts; that is, that he should be their king.

Their feeling toward the King of Zion is, "we will not have this man to reign over us." They are not endeavoring to do the will of God; they are not laboring to induce others to do it. How, then, can they expect to be heard, when they ask personal favors? If you would offer up acceptable prayer, you must pray after the manner our Savior taught us. Personal consideration must be subordinated to, and merged in, the great interests of the kingdom of God.

It is peculiarly appropriate that the petition we are now considering, should have been immediately preceded by the one to which your attention was called in a previous lecture.

We pray here for life, to which we all cling with such an unyielding grasp. Yet we should ever say with reference even to this, "thy will be done." And the great reason why we should wish to live is, that we may do the will of our Father in Heaven. And when we have finished the work he gives us to do, we should be ready, nay, glad to go home.

The direct teachings of this petition are highly important. The first which occurs to me is, our entire dependence upon God, even for the commonest comforts of life. Our Savior does not teach us to say, "Give us this day our daily bread," because this is the only thing for which we need to ask. But he takes out this from the circle of our wants, as the symbol, the representative of the whole. And it is worthy of note, that he singles out that in which we seem to be most independent. In what do we see more clearly the direct, simple result of our own labor, than in the procuring and preparation of our food? Yet even in this we are to recognize the hand of God. What he gives us, we gather; he opens his hand and satisfies the desire of every living thing. And if this be true of such apparently simple processes as the supply of our daily wants, how much more should we feel our dependence upon God for those things over which it is obvious we have no control, or at best but a limited and indirect one.

But there is a deep philosophy in this prayer, simple as it may seem; nay, silly, as I presume it must appear to the scornful, scoffing, godless man, who casts off fear, and restrains prayer before God. What a circle of agencies must be at work with unwearied diligence to provide my daily food. For me the sun must shine, and the rain must fall, the grass must grow, and the little brook must warble on its silvery way. The sturdy woodman must wield his axe. The sun-browned farmer must follow his plough, scatter the seed, and wave the gleaming sickle. The ship must spread her canvas to the breeze, the merchant-prince must build his ware-houses and his docks.

Well may I ask God to give me my daily food, when at so many points in this chain of events he can come in to derange every plan, to thwart every enterprize. He can send incessant rain and sweeping floods, or long-burning drought. He holds the winds in his fist, he can vex the ocean, and strew the sea-shore with wrecks. Almost every paper you pick up at the present time has something to say of the prospects of the wheat crop.* What does this mean?

* This Sermon was preached just before harvest.

Man has done all he can, and now he waits the pleasure and the providence of God. The prospect is fair now, they say, for a good return, but how soon may this fair prospect be blasted. How appropriate, how philosophical, then, is this prayer.

But we are not taught to ask for our food in the gross, if I may use such an expression. We do not say, once for all, "Give us every day our daily bread, so that we have a supply of food for a long time to come;" but every day we come and say, "Give us this day our daily bread." In the parallel passage, in Luke, it is said, "Give us, day by day, our daily bread;" thus we recognize God's ever-present agency. We are not to suppose that he interferes only at some remote point, and at longs intervals; that only the hidden and perhaps inscrutable laws which regulate the wind blowing where it listeth, and similar operations in nature, are under the control and guidance of the Almighty, but the apparently trivial circumstances which enter into the details of every day, are alike subject to his power, and watched over by his eye.

This brings me to formally assert, what a careful observer will have inferred from what has been already said, that this petition involves and teaches, what is commonly called the doctrine of a particular providence. In other words, I believe, in the language of our Shorter Catechism, that "God's works of providence are his most holy, wise, and powerful, preserving and governing all his creatures, and all their actions." No other belief seems to me scriptural or rational And first let us appeal to the word and the testimony. What saith the Scripture? I take a few passages from the Old and New Testaments, as specimens of what may be found, as every body knows, in all parts of both. "He giveth to the beast his food, and to the young ravens which cry."—Psalm 147: 9. "He causeth the grass to grow for the cattle, and herb for the service of man, that he may bring forth food out of the earth."—Ps. 104: 14. "O Lord, thou preservest man and beast."—Ps. 36: 6. "He maketh his sun to rise on the evil and on the good, and sendeth rain on the just and on the unjust."—Matt. 5: 45. "Behold the fowls of the air: for they sow not, neither do they reap, nor gather into barns, yet your Heavenly Father feedeth them."—Matt. 6: 26. "Are not two sparrows sold for a farthing, and one of them shall not fall to the ground without your Father.* But the very hairs of your head are all numbered."—Matt. 10: 29, 30. If men would only receive the teachings of God's word,

* Not without your Father's notice, as it is often quoted; but without him, without his permission, his interposition.

we should have little dispute about a particular providence.

I said, however, that no belief but ours appeared rational to me, and here the hardest battle is to be fought in behalf of this doctrine. Many a man, who is compelled to acknowledge that the Bible teaches it, will yet demur as to its reasonableness. Paul, who was no mean logician, seems to have thought this a rational belief. For in his masterly address to the Athenians, in which he adduces no authority from Scripture, and was by the very nature of the case precluded from adducing any, but makes his appeal directly to the reason and conscience of his hearers, he makes this assertion: "God, that made the earth, and all things therein, hath made of one blood all nations of men, for to dwell on all the face of the earth, and hath determined the times before appointed, and the bounds of their habitation. For in him we live, and move, and have our being." How confidently he says this, as if anticipating no denial. How natural such a belief. Who can think that God would set in action all the mighty agencies at work around us in nature, and not superintend them? Who can think that he would create such beings as we are, with all our varied interests and wants, yet disregard us entirely. I for one cannot believe such an absurdity, such horrid impiety.

We are met here by a philosophical theory which seems to avoid this folly, yet denies, in terms, at least, a particular providence. Most of those who hold it, I think, profess to receive the Scriptures of the Old and New Testament as the word of God; but I am not aware that they ever undertake to prove it by the Bible.

This forbearance on their part is wise; for not only can it not be proved by Scripture, but when fairly analysed, when followed out to its legitimate results, it contradicts Scripture.

The devout Christians, who hold this theory, and there are not a few of them, have such confused views of it, that they do not perceive this contradiction. If they could only have clear, well-defined conceptions of what they now hold so vaguely, they would renounce it intellectually, as they actually do in their prayers and their emotions.

The theory referred to is, that "God at first imparted certain powers to the material and spiritual creation, and established certain permanent laws, and that, as he originally established this perfect order, this system of powers and laws, and set things in operation upon this plan, there is no need of his continued and present agency; that the created system thus contrived and established will go on of itself, without being constantly propelled, as they express it, by the hand of the Creator; that the powers or active principles with which he has endowed the system of things, and to which he has given perpetuity, continue to operate and produce their proper effects without any further act of divine power."* They compare the universe to a clock, or a similar piece of machinery, which, when wound up, goes of itself for a certain time. This theory, when fully carried out, turns God out of the universe; it does not see God anywhere; it never says, "*Lo! what hath God wrought.*" I say it never says this, because, if the universe came from the hand of God perfect, completely endowed with all these powers and agencies, there is no need for him ever to interfere. A clock must be wound up, but this is owing to its imperfections. If the universe is a vast clock, it never needs winding up or rearranging. Perfection is impressed upon every part of it. Where is the evidence of any occasional interference on the part of the Creator? Do the planets run their course at a constantly slackening pace? Does the thunder sound less and less loudly until the spring is again recoiled as tightly as before? There are some who believe that God does not interfere; he simply superintends; he watches over this vast and complicated machinery, lest some part of it should become deranged. But I

* Wood's Theological Lectures.

say to this, that if the mechanism is perfect, if these laws are as immutable as they say they are, there is no need of this. Who would think of sending for the maker of a clock to watch it all the time, lest it should get out of order? This would be proof, not that his mechanism was imperfect, but that it was a miserable failure. For my own part, if I held this theory at all, I would hold it in all its blank, naked, atheism, that God set the universe a going, and since then has never touched a single spring, has never spent a single thought upon it.

This is intelligible and consistent. There are some who say that God upholds the powers and laws of nature. It is very important to know what is meant by upholding. If it is meant that, God is always present, ensuring the efficiency of these powers, and securing the permanence of these laws, then this is all that we who believe in a particular providence contend for. We believe that he endowed the creation with certain powers, that he ordained certain modes in which these powers should act, that he is every where present, supporting these powers, and that they derive their strength immediately from him. Or if I were to state the matter exactly as it lies in my own mind, I should say that God determined to exert his power in certain uniform modes, and this is what I understand by a law of nature.

And he works through second causes, through the energies of nature, and the activity of man. To me it is no rhapsody of poetry that "sees God in clouds, and hears him in the wind." He is there to me. I see no blind impersonal law, but my Father's hand drawing the curtains of the night about me, and fanning my feverish cheek with the cooling breeze.

There is a variation of this clock theory, if it is not an entirely new one, which I must notice. It is a belief that ordinarily God lets the world go on according to general laws, without paying any attention to it, but in certain great crises he interferes. The rising of the sun, the falling of rain, the death of man, all these come to pass through the operation of permanent laws. But such great events as the downfall of an empire, the birth of Christ, the Great Reformation, are objects of his providential care.

This is, it seems to me, the most illogical of all the theories on this subject. For a care of one of these great events, involves a care over every thing connected with and related to it. And then let any one consider upon what little things great events sometimes hinge, how the circumstances of our daily life are interwoven with all the great movements of the age, and he will see that such a general providence, without a particular providence, is impossible. There are some things in regard to this matter I could wish to discuss more fully. One is the *animus*, the spirit, the intention, of this theory. It is evidently an attempt to save the Almighty the trouble, the effort of taking care of the universe.

Another point is the strange misconception of a law of nature, what it is and what it can do, that lies at the basis of this theory. I shall have occasion to recur again to the latter point, before I close this series of Sermons, and hope to have more time for its discussion.

But even then I know I shall find that this whole subject is in some of its aspects incomprehensible. Indeed, as Mr. Burke has said, "What subject is there, that does not branch out into infinity?" I must be permitted to add, before closing this brief and imperfect discussion, what is to me, however it may affect others, an unanswerable argument. The Bible is clearly opposed to the philosophical theory we have been considering. I have already referred to some of these passages. "He clothes the lilies, feeds the ravens, numbers the very hairs of our heads." The whole tenor of Scripture is to recognize the present, personal agency of God in all our life. We are told that this is a Hebrew form of speech. It is a form of speech I could wish to see pervade all languages. And let me say here, that on no other theory but that of a particular providence, is it possible to pray the prayer our Lord teaches us here. If he has no agency in the matter, why ask him to give us our food? Men of the world do not believe he has any such agency, and therefore they never ask him for such favors; they never thank him for what they have. But, my Christian friends, this is not our belief. We look upon our Heavenly Father as the author of all our mercies, and the God of all grace. We go out in the morning, assured that the steps of a good man are ordered by the Lord,—what he gives us, we gather. We come home at night, and he giveth his beloved sleep. Is not this a consoling doctrine? Who would not rather believe that this vast fabric of the universe is presided over by a conscious, intelligent person, capable of being moved by prayer, governing, it is true, according to great principles invariable within certain limits, yet so governing as that the poor and the helpless may hope for mercy; who would not rather believe this, than that we are under the dominion of blind, impersonal agencies, the control of which God has voluntarily abdicated?

This philosophical theory which some have attempted to hold at the same time with the Bible, gives us up as fully to Fatalism, as Mohammedism itself. True, order, of which they have made a god, reigns in their universe; but it is the order of despotism; it is the order which reigned in Warsaw, amid the shrieks and groans of the dying. From such order I turn away with horror, while I fix my eyes with grateful adoration on my Father in Heaven, whose kingdom ruleth over all.

Another lesson which our Lord teaches us in this petition, is the duty of family religion. We are, every family apart, to say, every morning, "Give us this day our daily bread." If I know my own heart, I love the public assemblies of the saints. I am not only willing, or even pleased, I delight to praise God in the great congregation. I hope, too, that it fills my soul with joy to meet with an individual Christian, to talk with him of our conflicts here, and of the glory that shall be revealed in us. But no department of the service of God is so attractive to me as family religion. How beautiful, for instance, to see a mother telling her children of Samuel, to whom God called when but a child; or of Him who said, "Suffer little children to come unto me;" or teaching them this prayer, which should be among the first things a mother teaches her child, and which should blend in with, and irradiate with its heavenly light, every memory of home. Especially, how sweet to gather your own little group, no traitor heart within that circle, no suspicious eye, no jarring voice; and say together, "Give us this day our daily bread; be our God and guide, our portion and hope." I pity the home where the voice of prayer is never heard—where they sit down to their daily food without thanking God. They may live in splendor and luxury, their tables may groan with abundance, and be graced with the delicacies of every season and every clime; but they know nothing of the purer joys of life. They have no idea how it sweetens every joy, and lightens every grief, to see in them all, the hand of our Heavenly Father. I would rather dwell in a hovel, and live on bread and water, loving and worshiping the Giver of every good and perfect gift, than to share in their golden wealth. And what an unwelcome visitor is the King of Terrors to such a family. No one to pray, no one to whisper in the ear of the dying that message of our Lord: "He that believeth in me, though he were dead, yet shall he live." O, what a dreary place is a prayerless home in the hour of affliction.

There may be some members of this Church, who are not in the habit of saying, "Give us this day our daily bread," who excuse themselves in various ways from this duty of family worship. I will not taunt you as men of the world do, with not being what professors of religion should be. But let me tell you kindly, that you are not only giving the enemy occasion to blaspheme, but you are depriving yourselves of an important source of strength and enjoyment.

I know of nothing, except secret prayer, which I hope none of you neglect, that will help you in the conflict with "corruption without, and temptation within," which is our common lot, so much as girding on afresh every day the whole armor of God, in the midst of those with whom you are most intimately associated, and who look up to you as their head. It would require a volume to discuss all the influences and relations of this delightful exercise. Let me simply suggest to you, that the machinery of your home life will move with less friction, and be less likely to get out of order, if you are in the habit of thus commending yourselves, as a family, to that God who setteth the solitary in families. And I must tell you frankly, that in refusing to worship him as a family apart, you are guilty of great injustice to your children. You are depriving them of one of the strongest safe-guards against vice and crime, with which they could be provided. I speak from experience, when I say that there is nothing will so powerfully restrain a young man, will so follow him into every haunt of sin, however gay and delusive, as the memory of a prayer a mother taught him, and a father offered up for him in the home of his childhood.

If, then, you would keep your children from

the evil that is in the world, accustom them from their earliest infancy to the delightful duties of family worship. And I think I may press this point upon irreligious parents. It seems to me you cannot begin the day better than by offering up the petition we are now considering, even though you have no such sense of guilt as would lead you to go on to the next one, "Forgive us our debts." Even if you think you are good enough, and do not feel any need of pardon, you are not so irrational as to deny that it is God who gives us rain from heaven, and fruitful seasons, filling our hearts with food and gladness."

Are you so ungrateful as to be ashamed to acknowledge his goodness even in the privacy of your home? The least that you can do with your meagre religious views is, to thank God every time you partake of his bounty. Do not, I beg you, with besotted, base ingratitude, cram yourself, and blaspheme your feeder.

Our Lord teaches us in this petition to avoid anxiety and fretfulness. We are not to look forward into the far-off future, when we pray for the supply of our temporal wants, but simply to ask for daily bread, and be satisfied with the assurance, that our Heavenly Father will give it.

Even Christians sometimes distress themselves with fears lest the time may come when they shall suffer want. But we are expressly forbid den to take such anxious thoughts for the morrow, seeing that our Heavenly Father knoweth what things we have need of. We have the promise of this life as well as of that which is to come. Why should we be disquieted? "I have been young," says the Psalmist, "and now am old; yet I have not see the righteous forsaken, nor his seed begging bread." Have prudence and foresight; but do not vex yourself about the future. That was a noble saying of the Christian hero: "I am immortal till my work is done."

We are also taught here to take heed, and beware of covetousness. Having food and raiment, let us be therewith content. He who prays this prayer cannot be a grasping, miserly man. Not that he will be content to live from "hand to mouth;" he will be more diligent and hopeful in his worldly business, since he here asks God to bless him in it. But he will ever remember, that all these things perish with the using; and that anything more than a supply of our wants, is valuable only as it enables us to minister to the spiritual and temporal necessities of others. He will, therefore, labor, as the apostle directs, "working with his hands the thing which is good, that he may have to give to him that needeth."

Finally, we are taught in this petition the brevity and uncertainty of life. I will not say to my soul, "soul, thou hast much goods laid up for many years; take thine ease, eat, drink and be merry," lest God should say to me, "Thou fool; this night thy soul shall be required of thee." I will only ask for daily food.

> "For here my spirit waiting stands,
> Till God shall bid it fly."

Blessed is that servant, whom his Lord, when he cometh, shall find so doing.

SERMON VI.

And forgive us our debts, as we forgive our debtors.
Matt. 6 : 12.

APPOLONIUS, of Tyranna, a heathen philosopher who lived shortly after Christ, was accustomed to pray, "Ye gods, give me only that which I deserve." There are few who could have the hardihood thus to address the Great Supreme.

Every religion of the race has recognized our condition as sinners, though they propose various and widely different methods of atoning for our sins. Indeed, a religion which did not, in some way, attempt to satisfy this craving of human nature after reconciliation with an offended Deity, could have no hold upon the soul of man. And just in proportion as this feeling is recognized and received, will be the power of a religious system. It is in this way we account for the fact that Unitarianism and Rationalism never have had, and never can have, such a wide and supreme dominion as Romanism. For the former, however plausible they may seem, and however much they may commend themselves to the mere intellect of man, lose their hold upon the heart, give the lie to his moral consciousness, by representing our estrangement from God as being very slight and unimportant, and our reconciliation to him as requiring little effort or sacrifice. But the latter, with all its absurdities and extravagancies, fully recognizes this longing of the soul for forgiveness, and attempts to relieve it. To this same source we trace the power of all false religions, and indeed, to a great extent, of all religions. The idolatrous Israelite made his child pass through the fire of Moloch; the Roman slaughtered whole herds in honor of his deities; the Hindoo swings from a hook, or flings himself under the wheels of the car of Juggernaut; the Romanist lacerates his body, or shuts himself up in a cell—because they believe these are the ways to expiate their sins, and obtain eternal life. The Christian differs from them, not as to the necessity of an atonement, or as to our offering some sacrifice to secure our restoration to favor, but he shows unto them a more excellent way.

Pure Christianity differs from all false religions, and from all imitations and corruptions of itself, in that it alone, properly speaking, teaches the doctrine of the forgiveness of sin. Other religions teach man's sinfulness, and the necessity of an atonement, but they devise methods by which man can make this expiation for himself, and thus demand, as a right, what the Gospel accords to him only as of the mercy of God.

It is Christianity alone which teaches us to confess, after we have done all, that we are but unprofitable servants; it is the Christian alone who cries, "God, be merciful to me a sinner." Yet there are those in every Christian community, the language of whose hearts, and a fair representation of whose belief is, "Give me that which I deserve." I do not suppose they would dare to frame such a prayer, or rather such a demand, into words, and address it to their Maker; yet their language and conduct show them to be disciples of Appolonius, rather than of Jesus. They are of the number of those who compare themselves among themselves. Our Savior spake a parable concerning them, describing them as those who trusted in themselves that they were righteous, and despised others. They are as good as Church members, or even better. They are taken for Church members, in preference to some who have really made a profession of religion. If ever they join the Church, they will be more consistent than Christians generally are. Oh, how different is this boastful spirit from that piteous cry, "God, be merciful to me a sinner!" which contrition wrings from the heart of the penitent.

And these persons are among the most unimpressible to whom the minister of the Gospel addresses himself. "Seest thou," said Solomon, "a man wise in his own conceit, there is more hope of a fool than of him." This is true, and was doubtless spoken in regard to the affairs of this life. But it has also a higher meaning and reference. The terms, wise and wisdom, fool and folly, are used, especially in the book of Proverbs, in a spiritual sense. "The fear of the Lord is the beginning of wisdom:" "Fools make a mock at sin." These, and similar expressions, show how we are to regard the passage I have quoted.— Seest thou a man wise in his own conceit—a man confident of his own goodness—wrapped up in the robe of his own righteousness, there is more hope of a fool, of a wicked man, than of him. Publicans and harlots press into the kingdom of God before proud, boastful Pharisees. The very beginning of a Christian life is a consciousness of our sinfulness in the sight of God; such a sense of our own unworthiness as makes us look with compassion on the faults of others, or lose sight of them entirely in the absorbing view of our own short comings. But these people, who run over all their good qualities so glibly: their kindness to the poor, their honesty, their correctness of life and speech, have no idea at all how their conduct must appear in the eyes of a holy God.

They cannot pray, "Forgive us our debts, our trespasses," for they imagine the few little slips they may occasionally make, are atoned for by their numerous good deeds. They do not feel their need of a Savior, and therefore the cross of Christ is foolishness to them. I should have more hopes of success with the wicked and the abandoned, than with those decent, well-behaved people who rely so much on their morality.

I would not deter men from being moral. I would not teach them that the more wicked they are the more hope is there of their being forgiven; and that therefore they should continue in sin, that grace may abound. God forbid! I would have all men to lead peaceable, and quiet, and honest lives.

But I would keep them from relying upon this outward morality for acceptance with God. I would have them consider how much of their goodness may be due to the force of circumstances—to the absence of temptation, or the fear of detection; and how little credit they deserve for such morality. Above all, I would have them beware how they venture to offer such seeming uprightness to Him who looketh on the thoughts and intents of the heart. I believe a virtuous person, who feels how little claim his goodness gives him upon the favor of God—is not far from the kingdom of heaven—is much more likely to turn to God, than a wicked man, with a benighted heart and a stupid conscience. But I assert again, that a man who relies upon his own goodness, is, so far as we can see, the most helpless of all. I should sooner expect the thief upon the cross, and the woman who was a sinner, to pray, "Forgive us our trespasses," than such proud, self-confident people.

I do not mean to say that all moral, upright persons, who have made no profession of religion, do thus plume themselves upon their supposed goodness. There are many of blameless lives, humanly speaking, who are far from trusting in themselves that they are righteous, and despising others. The Church of Christ loves and prays for such; nay, Christ himself beholding them, loves them. Yet it cannot be denied, that there are those in every Christian community, the language of whose heart is, "Give me what I deserve." And I say again, I have little hope of them: none at all until they are dislodged from their position of false security.

My Christian friends, there are just such self-righteous people in the Church, persons who trust in the soundness of their orthodoxy, the number and the fervor of their prayers—the punctuality of their attendance upon religious services, public or private.

And they, too, are the counterpart of our Savior's inimitable description. They not only trust in themselves that they are righteous, but they despise others. They look with ill-concealed contempt upon those whose creed is not so correct—whose devotions are not so frequent—whose gifts to missions and missionaries are not so numerous and costly. Here, again, I do not mean to depreciate orthodoxy, or attendance at meeting, or benevolence. They are important. I insist upon them as Christian duties, but I protest against a reliance upon them.

After we have done all, we should say, "we are unprofitable servants, we have done only what was our duty to do." Nothing is a better mark of a Christian, than lowliness of mind—a consciousness of our unworthiness. And there is nothing in which the religious experience of the day is more deficient. Read the writings of David, and Jeremiah, and Paul; examine the experience of Edwards, and of Brainard, and Martyn, and every eminent saint; and you will find them marked with this peculiarity, of a deep sense of sinfulness. What was said of different religions, may be said of the religions of different men. Just in preportion to the sincerity and strength of your consciousness of sin, will be the power and fervor of your Christian life. If you are one of those who think themselves very good members of the Church, you have great reason to stand in doubt of yourself. "Let him that thinketh he standeth, take heed lest he fall!"

The addition to this prayer, the condition annexed

to it by our Lord, is certainly a very marked peculiarity of our religion. Stoicism and Mahommedanism have taught men to treat with contempt the insults, and endure with patience the injuries they could not avenge, but they have never taught men to forgive. The very divinities of most religions have been passionate and revengeful, and of course their worshipers must have been like unto them. It is notorious, that men of the world look upon revenge, and implacability, as manly and honorable. Forgiveness is not even in the worldly man's catalogue of virtues; he never thinks of condemning himself for being harsh and unrelenting. In nothing does the Gospel of our Lord so set itself in opposition to the natural heart of man, as in this which Leighton calls the blessed doctrine of forgiveness. The utterances, to use a cant phrase of the day, of our Lord on this point, are clear and repeated. In this very sermon on the mount, from which the text is taken, this difficult and distasteful duty is enjoined no less than three times, with a plainness which cannot be evaded. In the preceding chapter, in exposing the false teaching of the Scribes and Pharisees, he says: "I say unto you, love your enemies, bless them that curse you, do good to them that hate you, and pray for them which despitefully use you and persecute you." In this petition we are now considering, he teaches the same great lesson. And, not content with this repetition, immediately at the close of this prayer, he recurs to this identical topic, saying, "For if ye forgive men their trespasses, your heavenly Father will also forgive you; but if ye forgive not men their trespasses, neither will your Father forgive your trespasses." So important did he consider this duty, which men of the world, and even some who call themselves his followers, feel at liberty to utterly ignore. And you will notice that, in this last repetition, our Lord makes our forgiveness to depend entirely on our forgiving others. Was there over such a religion? Was there ever such a prayer? "Forgive us our trespasses, as we forgive those who trespass against us."* There is no better, surer mark of a Christian, than the exhibition of a forgiving spirit. Better than offerings and whole burnt offerings, better than zeal and orthodoxy, it stamps its possessor as an Israelite indeed, in whom there is no guile. Yet we find not a few professed followers of our Savior, harsh and unrelenting: severe in their

* I have preferred, generally, in the course of this Sermon, to use the word trespass, instead of debts. The former term conveys, I think, a more correct idea of the real meaning, (see verse 14th of this Chapter,) of the text, though the words, debts and debtors, are literal translations from the original. Trespasses and trespass occur, however, in the parallel passage in Luke.

judgment of the erring, they seem to take a kind of demoniac delight in the anguish and remorse which the guilty themselves exhibit. They share in and rejoice at the scorn and contempt which society visits upon such persons; and with what quiet satisfaction they seem to be inspired, when some proud person of wealth or distinction falls, and is humbled to the dust. No grief, no regret even, only a cold, bitter, "served him right," or, "just what I expected." Is this a fancy sketch? I would that it were. But there are such people in every communion—professed imitators of Him who prayed, "Father, forgive them, for they know not what they do." Oh, my brethren, such a bitter, vindictive spirit, is a horrible caricature of our holy religion.

The world is often called unforgiving; and so it is, to particular classes. For the lowly and obscure, for the unfortunate and miserable, however penitent, however much a reformed and upright course of conduct may have atoned for early errors, for them there is no mercy. But if a man has wealth and assurance; if, so far from being penitent, the more guilty he is, the bolder he grows, the world will soon forget his offences. Nay, there are things, criminal even in the eye of human law, for which he may be applauded. And there is scarcely any offence he can commit, which, if he has wealth and station, the world will not ultimately forgive and forget. There is a singular exception to this rule, to which I wish to call your attention. The world has no mercy for an erring professor of religion, or ministers of the Gospel. They judge us with a rigorous severity, they could not endure themselves. Let them remember, that with what judgment they judge, they shall be judged; and with what measure they mete, it shall be measured to them. They sometimes undertake to justify their severity toward us by saying that they do not make such professions.

We do not, I would say in reply, profess to be perfect; we do not set ourselves up as models for imitation. We promise to endeavor to live godly in Christ Jesus; to adorn the doctrine of God our Savior, with well ordered lives and conversation. But there is nothing in this, coupled as it always is with an acknowledgment of our proneness to err, to justify such uncharitable severity as is generally exhibited toward us by the world. I, for one, am thankful that a merciful and gracions God is to be our final judge.

The natural disposition of woman is more congenial to the mild and peaceful spirit of the Gospel, than that of man. Christianity has done every thing for her, and she, in return, has done much for Christianity.

In almost every Church, a majority of the members are women. Our prayer-meetings throughout the world would make but a sorry show, if it were not for them. And the teachings of this prayer we are now considering, owe much of their influence to the fact, that it drops into our hearts in childhood, from a mother's lips. This particular petition is in sympathy with the general temper of woman. She is ordinarily more forgiving and compassionate than man. A passionate, revengeful woman is frightful. I love to see a lady have strength of soul enough to repel insult, and resist injury, but those "women of spirit," as they are often called, those viragoes, that bristle up every time their capricious fancy imagines any thing has been said or done which is not as deferential as it should be, are utterly intolerable. They are a libel on their sex. And you meet them in all ranks and grades of society, amid the tinsel and glare of fashionable life, as well as in the filth and crime of the dens of infamy. If these passionate, revengeful women—ladies I must not call them—are disgusting, a cold, hard, unrelenting woman is forbidding in the extreme. She is a moral ice-berg, chilling every thing that comes within the range of her influence. To the honor of the sex, let it be said, there are comparatively few such women. Most of them are ready to forgive injury, and forget unkindness.

Yet, such a bundle of inconsistencies is poor

human nature, that even here there is a singular exception. Though woman is thus naturally inclined to forgive, toward offenders of her own sex she exhibits an unsparing severity. She takes into account no mitigating circumstances, looks at no overwhelming power of temptation, no surprisal in an unguarded moment. She sees only the crime and the criminal, and on both she visits her weighty displeasure. No tears can wash away the guilt of the erring one; no subsequent good conduct can win for her again that place in the confidence of her sister, which, by one fatal misstep she forfeited,—and forfeited forever.

Man may be melted by her grief and anguish, he may be re-assured by her reformation, but gentle woman has for her always the same stony face, the same adamantine heart. This is true, generally, of all the offences by which woman loses her place in society. But there is a class of transgressions, or rather transgressors, in the treatment of whom woman is, in my judgment, peculiarly unjust. I know the morbid sensitiveness which rules our country would forbid my speaking on this topic. I can pay no deference to such mawkish delicacy. To the pure, all things are pure, and they who squirm most under what I am about to say, will be the most corrupt. I say, then, plainly, that woman has no charity for those of her sex, who offend against the great law of purity. Here, she never forgives, she never forgets. Let an unsuspecting girl yield to the wily arts of the seducer, and she is ruined forever. The brand is on her forehead, and nothing can efface it. But the vile betrayer, that villain of all villains, "earth's most abhorred, God's most abandoned, hell's most-damned," is received, aye, welcomed. Christian mothers,—I hope Christian fathers seldom do—but Christian mothers court for their daughters the society of these men, reeking with the filth of vice, and rotten to their very heart's core with corruption. But the poor, deluded victim, is driven out with the mark upon her forehead, deeper and blacker than that of Cain.

Now, if woman would be simply just, let her treat her betrayer as she treats his victim. Let her turn away from him with the same horror with which she shrinks from the touch of her erring sister. I may be mistaken in my belief that woman ought to treat the betrayed with more gentleness; but I do know that she sins greatly in smiling on the vile seducer. It is notorious, that these men are courted and flattered; that their awful crime is no barrier to their admission into good society. To me, such another villain as the betrayer of unsuspecting innocence, does not darken God's sunshine. Though he were my brother, nay, though God should curse me with a child so vile and profligate, I must shrink from him with horror.

It may be that, having been, by the Providence of God, in the very riot and hot-blood of youth, constituted the protector of an only sister, I feel too strongly on this point; but I must say, I have often thought, if there is any criminal for whom no city of refuge on earth should open its gates, on whom the law should visit its most unsparing severity, it is the seducer. Did I not know that God was omnipotent, I should almost doubt whether hell itself had a punishment that could parallel the enormity of such guilt.

But let us not forget who it is that has said, "Vengeance is mine, I will repay." And even this criminal, if he turn again, saying, "I repent," is to be forgiven. But this is not the way in which woman treats such offenders. She spurns her repentant sister, while she smiles upon the seducer; who not only shows no remorse, but even glories in the shame and disgrace of his victim. Gentle woman will link her fate with his for life, while she rejects with disdain the rough hand of the farmer or mechanic, who gains his livelihood by honest toil. Let her at least, with even-handed justice, commend the same bitter chalice to the lips of the betrayer; and, as the minister of him who said to a weeping penitent, "Neither do I condemn thee: go and sin no more," may I not go still further? This transaction I have just referred to, seems to me to have been left on record for the special purpose of silencing that prudish modesty, and rebuking that heartless severity, which turns away with contempt from an erring woman. He who did no sin, neither was guile found in his mouth, who was holy, harmless and undefiled; he could say, "Neither do I condemn thee: go and sin no more." Shall not, then, woman look with pity on her fallen sister? I do not ask for impunity to crime; I do not plead the cause of the bold and unabashed, who glory in their shame, and flaunt their crime in the open face of day. I do not say, let them be treated with the same respect as if there were no stain upon their character. May the time never come in American society, when a woman can be so false to every instinct of her sex—can so violate every obligation she owes to God and man, as to give herself up to the dominion of lust, and yet retain her place among her fellows.

But I plead for the poor creature, deceived and betrayed by a fiend in human shape. Give her a chance to redeem her character: say to her, as Jesus did, "Go, and sin no more." Do not drive her out to herd with the shameless and the abandoned. Remember this prayer of your childhood, "Forgive us our trespasses, as we forgive those who trespass against us."

I gladly turn away from this sad topic, with which we have seldom any particular concern, to remind you that our Lord here speaks of the forgiveness of offences personal to ourselves. "Forgive us our trespasses, as we forgive those who trespass against us."

Many a person who can, with comparative ease, overlook transgressions of the law of God or man, find it difficult, or, as they sometimes say, impossible, to forgive and forget those petty little offences which are every day committed against us individually. The disrespect, the rudeness, the harshness, the neglect, intentional or unintentional, with which he is treated, or fancies he is treated, rankles long in his heart.

Remember, my dear brother, for I cannot repeat this too often, that we are to forgive those who trespass against us. Especially would I press the lesson now, as we are on the eve of a great political excitement, as intense, perhaps, as any that have preceded it. Certainly the bitterness of sectional strife will be infused into the coming contest more largely than ever before.

It becomes every Christian, under such circumstances, to take heed to himself. Whichever side you may espouse, there are abundance of abusive epithets in store, and multitudes ready to apply them to you. Your Christian character may even be questioned, your motives aspersed, and you yourself accounted the filth and offscouring of the earth.

Do I therefore advise you to preserve a strict neutrality in the coming contest? I counsel you to no such moral cowardice. Wo to our nation, when abuse and slander can so terrify good men as to keep them from bringing their influence to bear upon its government. Choose your ground well and wisely, and then maintain it in the fear of God. "In your patience possess your souls." "See that none render railing for railing, but contrariwise." "Forgive those who trespass against you, as you would yourself be forgiven."

Though it does not come logically within the scope of my present discourse, let me entreat you to be careful lest you trespass against others. Be like the Psalmist of old, who purposed that his mouth should not transgress. Take heed to your ways, that you sin not with your tongue. Above all, let not alienation of heart invade the Church of God. Let the followers of Christ stand together, and say to the raging waters of clamor, and wrath, and bitterness, and evil speaking, thus far shall you go, and no farther.

I would have you notice particularly that our forgiveness of others, is to be the measure of our own: "As we forgive those who trespass against us." How important that when we pray this prayer, we know what we are saying. He who goes to God with a hard, relentless heart, asks his Heavenly Father to turn away from him with the same contemptuous disdain with which he rejects his fellow man. This prayer in the mouth of a revengeful, unforgiving person, is a most dreadful imprecation of God's righteous vengeance on himself. And be careful that the pardon you extend to others is not tardy and reluctant, wrung from you by many prayers and tears. Do not, as Lord Bacon says in one of his touching prayers, "Let the sun almost go down upon your wrath." Oh! if we who are here before God to-day would only go out into the world to exemplify the spirit of this prayer, what a change it would work in our lives, and in the lives of those around us; for seeing our good works, they would be won, by our good conversation, to glorify our Father in Heaven.

I have repeatedly called your attention to the correct philosophy of this prayer. I do not think it out of place to do so, for these things show that he who taught us this prayer, knew what was in man, and that his teachings harmonize with our daily experience. In reference to this petition, we can discern this harmony. Every careful observer must have remarked a deep and intimate connection between a sense of our own sinfulness, and a readiness to forgive others. Both in the Church and the world, the proud Pharisee, who trusts in himself, is most ready to despise others, and will treat them with the utmost severity. While on the other hand, he who is the most fully aware of his own unworthiness in the sight of God, is most ready to throw the mantle of charity over the failing of his fellows. Conscious that he himself owes the Master ten thousand talents, he cannot, especially if he feel that he has been freely forgiven, treat his brother roughly for a debt of a hundred pence.

We see in this the justice of our Savior's emphatic repetition, at the close of this prayer, of the sentiment of this particular request. "For if ye forgive not men their trespasses, neither will your Father forgive you." For the possession of this forgiving spirit is, as I have before remarked, one of the best possible evidences of a proper sense of our own great guilt, and such a sense of guilt will always teach one charity.

Finally, I would remark, that as the petition we last considered was peculiarly appropriate to the beginning of the day, this is equally so to its close. How eminently proper, when the harsh noises of the day are gone, and the silence and the calm of night come, that you should gather round your family altar, the loved and the loving, and say, "Forgive us our trespasses, as we forgive those who trespass against us."

Such be our practice and spirit, my fellow sinners, all needing every day forgiveness from God and from each other. Let not the sun go down upon your wrath. Let the lullaby that soothes your home to sleep, be that lyric of the Christian poet:

> "Forgive me, Lord, for thy dear Son,
> The ills that I this day have done;
> That with myself, the world, and thee,
> I, ere I sleep, at peace may be."

SERMON VII.

And lead us not into temptation.—Matt. 6 : 13.

Having prayed for forgiveness for the past, it is natural and proper that we should ask for security for the future. There is evidently need of this. The world is a scene of probation, and it is, of course, necessary that we should undergo some trials. We sometimes hear persons complain of God's testing the disposition of our first parents in the garden of Eden, but in no other way could their obedience have been shown. And the trial to which they were subjected was so simple and direct, it was so little that they were required to do, that we ought rather to admire the compassion of God than to complain of his injustice.

Temptation, the opportunity of doing wrong, is still necessary to the perfection of our character. We here pray that God will so arrange the future that we shall have no severer trial than is necessary for our good. We recognize and accept our probationary condition; but conscious of our frailty, we ask Him who knows our frame to remember that we are but dust, and not to suffer us to be tempted above what we can bear. And there is no impropriety in this; for we do not live under the rule of blind fatalism, but of a most holy, wise, and powerful Father, whose "eyes are over the righteous, and whose ears are open to their cry."

There is in this petition an implied, but none the less evident rebuke of that rash and reckless running in the way of temptation, from which so much mischief has flowed. Most people have such an entire confidence in their strength of purpose, that they do not hesitate, to put themselves in situations of great exposure. This is characteristic of men of the world, and of young men in particular. They are not afraid: they can take care of themselves. They can hang around groceries, and handle cards, and not become drunkards or gamblers. Alas! how many of these boastful youths find their way to the gutter and the dungeon. The ruin of thousands is owing to their failure to keep themselves, and to ask God to keep them, out of the way of temptation. Yet this failure is the natural result of their religions opinions; and is another evidence of the fact that a man's practice depends upon his belief. The current belief of the world is, that they can protect themselves,—that they do not need the help of God; and so they do not ask him not to lead them into temptation. Nay, they run greedily in the way of evil, never doubting their own powers. Ah! if they had only distrusted themselves, and gone to God for help, they would have proved the truth of that saying of the apostle, "When I am weak, then am I strong."

It may be well for any of you, who pride yourselves upon your morality, who are sure of your ability to take care of yourselves, from the fact that you have kept yourselves pure hitherto; it may be worth while for any of you here, who rely upon your own morality, to inquire how much of this goodness is owing to God's having, unasked, kept you out of the way of temptation. You are, we will suppose, and I would not bate the tithe of a hair from your virtues, you are honest in all your dealings, owing no man, defrauding no man. But will you dare to say that if you had been tempted more severely, you would not have fallen. Perhaps you have never been in real pressing need of money, with an opportunity of obtaining it by dishonest or dishonorable means, and do not know how the cries of wife and children, and the fear of want, may goad one on to frenzy. You are moral and virtuous. But you have always been shielded from fierce assaults of the tempter. Can you take any credit to yourself for this accidental goodness? Ought you not rather to praise God, to whose mercy you owe it all? For my own part, I do not hesitate to say, with the great apostle, By the grace of God I am what I am. I can see many a point at which I might have turned aside to irretrievable ruin, had not his

> "Arm unseen, conveyed me safe,
> And led me up to man."

The theology of the world, their views of man's dependence upon God, and God's control over man, being such, it is not to be wondered at that they are rash and self-confident. But the Church, amid all her diversities, has recognized, at least in her devotions, God's control of our feelings and actions. It is a peculiar doctrine of our Church, at least it is so considered, that God has such control over us, that we may properly pray, "Lead us not into temptation;" and that we are so enfeebled, so prone to evil, that we need to avoid, so far as the providence of God will allow, all occasion of sin. Yet there are many among us, who, though they say, and perhaps really ask, "Lead us not into temptation," do yet, by their neglect of that other saying of our Lord, "Watch and pray, lest ye enter into temptation," betray a great want of that consciousness of weakness, which alone can give earnestness to the petition we are now considering. The reason why we are reckless in exposing ourselves, and at the same time so cold and formal in our prayers, that God would not lead us into temptation is, that we have too much confidence in our own strength. We are all naturally inclined to make this sad mistake. But I think youthful Christians, and Christians in the beginning of their religious life, are most apt to fall into it. Persuaded of their ability to carry out their resolutions, or at least over confident, they do not feel the necessity of surrounding themselves with every defence, of putting on the whole armor of God, and avoiding every unnecessary temptation.

To you who are in the beginning of your Christian life, I would say, you need every source of strength within your reach. Daily prayer to God, daily reading and meditating upon his word, conversation with the devout as often as practicable, and the social prayer meeting, you ought by no means to neglect. Do not, I beseech you, follow the evil and dangerous example of those who, older in life and religious profession, grieve the hearts of their pastor and fellow Christians, as well as weaken their own spiritual strength, by neglecting these means of grace. And do not go unnecessarily in the way of temptation. Do not find your friends and associates exclusively or principally among the worldly-minded and irreligious. Do not seek your pleasures ordinarily in places where it is understood that religion is a forbidden topic, or among those who are in the habit of treating it lightly. Such a course is exceedingly dangerous. Many a young Christian, who set out with every prospect of leading a holy life, and who did run well for a time, has in this way gone back, and walked in the ways of God no more; or has degenerated into a mere professor of religion, regular at church and at the communion table, but known at no other place, and recognized in no other manner as a servant of the Lord.

But if you should not come to such a sad end as this, by neglecting to watch and pray lest you enter into temptation, you may well fear that God will lead you into it as he did David and Peter, to show you your own weakness. To cure you of your over-confidence, he will let you fall into some great, and it may be, disgraceful sin. And with all your care and prudence, you will be subjected to trials enough to test your virtue. You need not, for instance, seek the society of passionate and insulting people to prove your control over your own temper. You will have opportunities enough of showing this, with every lawful and Christian precaution you may take to avoid contact with wicked and unreasonable men.

> "Seek not temptation, then, which to avoid,
> Were better——trial will come unsought.
> Would'st thou approve thy constancy,
> Approve first thy obedience."

There is no class of persons to whom this prayer is more appropriate than to parents. No one can tell the fate of the children you are training up. However long you may be spared, and however carefully you may guard them, the time will come when you must send them out into the world to fight for themselves the battle of life. And there is not on the records of human guilt a solitary sin into which your children may not fall. The men and women, for there are both, now dwelling lonely and apart in dungeons, or herding together in the haunts of vice and crime, were some of them the children of pious parents, though most of them came from such prayerless homes as I fear many of you inhabit. The assassin, whose very name thrills your soul with horror, was once a little child, as peaceful and happy as any of yours. Your boy, whose bright eye and beaming face give promise of a noble manhood, may live only to bring down your gray hairs with sorrow to the grave, or to burden you with a heart that, like a bruised reed, is waiting to be broken. Your daughter may find her dwelling-placc for life in—

"——those homes of sin and shame,
Where Satan shows his cloven foot,
But hides his titled name."

How, then, should you pray to God not to lead them into temptation, lest they be tempted above what they can bear. And I would, in reference to this topic, address myself particularly to irreligious fathers. Most men prefer that the mother of their children should be devout and pious. Indeed, many profane, ungodly men glory not a little in the religion of their wives. They would be shocked at the thought of these latter being the same sneering, blasphemous skeptics they are themselves. They feel, and they are right, that humble, unaffected piety, is the crowning grace of woman's character; that their homes are safer for the religion of their wives. They feel that their children will be more likely to be brought up so they shall not disgrace the name they bear. But while they thus value the piety of their wives, they themselves cast off fear, and restrain prayer before God, or it may be, are profane and vicious.

I shall not stop here to show how honorable it is to be a Christian, nor to expose the mistake of those who think it unmanly to pray and read the Bible. I simply content myself now with assuring irreligious men that their children need their prayers and their protection. They need every breast-work that can be thrown up around them—every barrier that can be interposed between them and evil. The prayers and teachings of their mothers may do much, weakened though they be by your conversation, and contradicted by your practice. But how much more might they effect if seconded by your prayers and example. Can you think of letting your children grow up in a world so full of snares and dangers, without often asking God to shield and guide them?

But if we thus condemn those who, with all their watching, fail to pray, what shall we say of parents who neither watch nor pray, or who destroy the efficacy of their prayers by their heedlessness? How shall we find language strong enough to condemn those whose boys roam our streets at will, learning all the filth and blasphemy that even Sodom knew, making night hideous with their noise, and the day loathsome with their oaths and vulgarity? What can we say to the mothers who never know, and it would seem never care, what books their daughters read, what company they keep? Who deck them in costly finery, and send them, or weakly suffer them, to force their way into the ball-room, where sometimes the dance is too lascivious to be thought of in this sacred place, and where always the mother cannot tell how polluted may be the hand her daughter will clasp, or how treacherous the arm upon which she will lean? How can such parents pray for their children, or with them, at the family altar, "lead us not into temptation?" I cannot believe they often do.

There is a mistake sometimes made by parents in another direction, though not so common, nor by any means so dangerous as the guilty heedlessness which we have been considering. It is shutting up their children as far as possible from all intercourse with others, never letting them go from under the eye of their parents or some superior, and thus keeping them in profound ignorance of the world and its snares. But this makes their moral character too frail and delicate for use. Robustness of soul must be obtained in the same way with that of the body, by exercise. You would not coop your child up in a hot room and wrap him up in blankets, for fear he would take cold, and thus make him almost certain to, whenever a clear, strong breeze blows on him. You would not keep him from moving a muscle, for fear he should dislocate his arm, or sprain his ankle, and thus render sure his breaking down entirely when any moderate exertion was absolutely required of him. Do not, then, prohibit your children from all intercourse with other children. Choose for them the best companions, just as you would choose the safest sports and employments; for they will learn evil enough from them. And remember that you are to choose for them, and not they for themselves. Do not keep them always in your sight, but give them the best instruction you can; and then send them out to practice on it, praying God to keep them. Do not, like the half-drowned foolish fellow in the Greek fable, vow they shall not touch the water until they have learned to swim; but teach them to swim, and give them trusty companions, and you have done your part to keep them from going down into the depths of infamy that underlie the sea of life. God will hear your prayers and do his.

Cultivate in your children the habit of confiding in you, telling you what they see and hear, that you may teach them to discriminate between good and evil. It is painful to think what a chasm generally yawns between the child and its parents; how much evil the former is learning, and sometimes in utter ignorance of its dangerous tendency; while the latter are equally ignorant that their child is receiving such instruction, simply because this confiding disposition has never been cherished. Children should be brought up, and they may be, to tell their parents whatever transpires in their intercourse with others, and to understand that whatever they are told not to tell to their parents is certainly wrong. And if, in spite of all your care, or which is far more likely, through your carelessness, you have a child that will conceal from or deceive you, I charge you solemnly in the sight of God to break up that habit, at whatever cost. No surer basis could be laid for the ruin of your child. He or she will be like the apples of Sodom, fair without, but rottenness within. They will keep you in ignorance of their evil courses, while rumor, with her hundred tongues, publishes them on every street and in every corner. It is sad to think, to how many Christian fathers and mothers the knowledge of their children's sins comes, alas! too late, like a thunderbolt from a clear sky, simply because they have never accustomed their children to tell what they saw and heard. While they slept, the enemy sowed tares in the hearts of their sons and daughters.

Another capital mistake in this hot-bed moral culture, and I have already alluded to it, is keeping children in profound ignorance of the world and its snares. This is done by some parents through guilty carelessness. They never find time; they are too busy making money or dresses; they cannot stop to talk about such things. But those to whom I now address myself, do it from mistaken care. They fear that they shall thus give their children a knowledge of evil they would not otherwise acquire, and so lead them into temptation. You may be sure they will learn enough of such things long before people would generally suspect them; and the wisest thing you can do is to forestall the devil and his agents. I have no doubt it is your duty to inform your children to some extent of the ways of the world. Yet it is difficult to say precisely how far you ought to go in this. There are, unquestionably, forms and phases of vice of which they had better be entirely ignorant. Such books as the "Pirate's Own Book," confessions of murderers, and the "Hot Corn Stories," which some misguided religious people have praised, ought to be prohibited to children, because they familiarize them with a grade of society and a kind of life of which they had better never dream. The man who takes his children frequently to the brothel, the gambling hell, or the circus, or is always talking of the scenes there enacted, and describing them with great accuracy, does his children much harm. He makes them fully acquainted with that of which the less they know the better.

> "Vice is a monster of such frightful mien,
> That to be hated, needs but to be seen;
> But seen too oft, familiar with her face,
> We first endure, then pity, then embrace."

Yet fore-warned is fore-armed; and you will make a sad mistake, if you do not put your child on his guard against the snares that will beset his daily path.

I would especially press this duty upon mothers; for I fear they greatly neglect it. What I have said of the general topic applies to this particular point. You need not fear giving your daughters a knowledge of evil, which they would acquire in no other way. They will certainly learn from others, sooner or later, and generally long before you suspect. You are in little danger in beginning too early. Talk to them kindly and plainly, delicately of course. A woman should never talk otherwise, even to her own sex. To thus guide and instruct your daughters is not merely advisable, it is a solemn duty, which you ought, on no account, and for no pretext, to neglect. Many a poor girl, by such timely precaution, might have been saved from hopeless ruin.

Bear with me while I apply the general principles I have laid down, to a particular topic, in regard to which I am often consulted. Some parents refuse to send their children to school at home, and many hesitate about sending them abroad. It is, I acknowledge, a dangerous experimont in either case. I saw so much, during five years' experience as a teacher, of the corrupting influence of passionate, ill-governed children upon those who had been better trained, even when the latter were still under the eye of their parents, during their leisure hours, that I was for a long time of the opinion that where parents could give any tolerable kind of instruction to their children, they had better not send them to school. But I am inclined to reverse that decision; for much is gained by the contact of mind with mind. Children learn so much faster when grouped together; and the school is a little world; they meet there, on a small scale, the very forces they must encounter; they acquire the very powers of resistance they will need in after life; and so I would send them to school, taking the following precautions. Do not send them too early. Let them be at least seven years old, so that their character shall have acquired some force and consistence. Give them, up to that time, as far as possible, a correct moral training. Habituate them to telling you what is said and done by their playmates at school. Do not leave it for chance to bring out the wickedness they may have witnessed, but let them be so accustomed to confide in you, that they will think of nothing but telling you. Send them to a good teacher. Beware of the paltry economy of seeking the cheapest. Send them to a teacher who will watch over their morals, and guard with sleepless vigilance against every influence that would corrupt them, if you can find such an one. I know such teachers are like angels' visits, not only because they are few and far between, but because they are angels of mercy to your children. Their price is above rubies,—silver should not be weighed for the price thereof. Observe your children when at home; narrowly but not suspiciously. Watch for the rising scab of any moral leprosy, that you may check it at the outset.

After a child has been thus sent to school at home till he is at least fourteen or fifteen, I see nothing wrong, indeed it is sometimes advisable, to send him abroad, taking similar precautions. Send him to a good teacher, good in the sense I have already referred to. Provide for him a cheerful home among the devout. Secure him, so far as practicable, good companions. Accustom him still to tell you what his associates and amusements are. Observe him when at home, and strive to stop every beginning of evil. Above all, throughout his whole career, at home and abroad, pray often, and teach him to pray, "lead us not into temptation." Again I say, you have done your part. God will hear your prayers and do his. Shall he not hear his own elect, who cry day and night unto him, though he bear long with them?

Let me say, before I leave this subject, see to it that whatever instruction you give, be it less or more, is correct. Do not give your children false views of life, or endeavor to found their opposition to evil on false grounds. If you send them away to school, do not lead them to suppose that those who mislead them will be the rude and ragged loafers on the streets, or that it is the low groceries they must avoid, but that the saloons and oyster-cellars are the most dangerous places; and that the young and lively who are themselves on the road to ruin, are the most dangerous companions. Beware of inoculating them with your own unfounded prejudices. If you would keep them out of the ball-room, and you all know that I think it a dangerous place, do not teach them to look upon dancing as an awful crime, or to suppose that they will meet in the ball-room only with repulsive people. But let them know that such midnight orgies are ruinous to the health of their bodies; that disregard of God and dislike of religion reign there; and that above all, the seducer prowls there for his victim. Would you inspire them with disgust towards the circus? It is the most proper feeling they could have. Do not represent it to them as some huge, misshapen creature like the Centaur of the Greek mythology, with the head of a man ending in the body of a horse. Let them know something about it. You might even permit them to see its glare and tinsel; you might refresh them with the coarse, vulgar wit of the clown, and the delicate attitudes of the immaculate artists. But teach them that the Masters and Misses who perform these surprising feats are either children kidnapped from their parents, or homeless orphans, picked up on the street and compelled, by brutal cruelty, to amuse parents and children who come from homes generally of happiness and sometimes of refinement, to witness the sport. Teach your daughters what monsters of vice these vagabond showmen are, how utterly unworthy to minister to the amusement or receive the applause of a virtuous woman.

Would you guard them against the seductive influences of card-playing? It is desirable that you should. Do not make them believe that it is a sin to know one card from another, or that no one but vile and abandoned people play. Do not teach them to be afraid of their pocket-book in the company of all who play. They will soon learn that this is all a mistake. Take them into the gambling-hell, show them the haggard face and blood-shot eye of the ruined man. Tell them that the fierce, desperate men around them began their career by playing with a sister or a friend; that fair, white hands wove the first meshes of the net in which they are entangled. Let your children know that though there is no sin in handling cards, yet he who begins, can never tell where he will end. To say the *least*, he puts himself in the way of danger; he plays with an *asp*, and lays his hand on a cockatrice's den. Do you wish they may never contract the vile habit of theatre-going, by which so many young people have been ruined. I do not say you should take them there once, and when they have seen all its apparent splendor, that you should then unveil to them the corruption and vice, which I will not say sleep, but rather riot beneath. Many judicious people think this is the best way. I have not yet made up my mind that you should go that far, but I do say, whatever you tell them, let it be the truth. Do not let them imagine a theatre is a hideous place, full of fierce men and coarse, ill-mannered women, lest if they ever are decoyed in there, as some time or other they will be very likely to be, and find a fine, large room, flooded with light, and filled with fashionably-dressed, apparently respectable, quiet, well-behaved people, they will think their pious old father and mother were very good, well meaning sort of people, but they were sadly ignorant what a nice place a theatre was, or they never would have said so much against going there. If you would save your children from the evil that is in the world, especially from those forms of it to which I have just alluded, (and surely there is no Christian parent here, to say the least, who does not,) teach them that card-playing is the most successful snare, and the circus and the theatre are the favorite hunting ground of the thief, the gambler, of her whose steps take hold on hell, and of every other recruiting officer of the great enemy of God and man.

The question is often asked, why so many

children of pious parents, and especially of ministers, who seem to have been trained up in the way they should go, do yet depart from it. This is owing, of course, to a variety of causes. One of them, and a prominent one is, I think, that the false views of the danger I have been condemning are inculcated upon them. This is done with the best of intentions, no doubt, but its effects are none the less injurious. These young people find that their parents were mistaken—that the ball-room, the theatre, and a game of cards are very different things from what they were taught to suppose. And some of them never discover what the real dangers are, until they are given up entirely to the power of evil habits. Though a majority of them, I believe, sated with these frivolities, finding them not at all to be compared with the pure and peaceful pleasures of a pious home, do at last return to the shepherd and bishop of their souls. Let Christian parents know whereof they affirm, if they would keep their children out of temptation.

If there is any character who resembles the devil, it is the tempter. He who would, for the sake of gain or gratification, deliberately lead his fellow men into evils is essentially fiendish. It makes little difference in his guilt, and none at all in the results, whether he does it without thinking; he ought to think. When this prayer, "lead us not into temptation," is addressed to men; when they see that in the providence of God, the virtue and happiness of their fellow creatures are to a greater or less extent in their power; ought they not to take heed to these things? Do you say this prayer cannot be addressed to men? It often is, and alas! is often disregarded. It comes to-day to you who are young, from those pious parents whose children you are teaching to desecrate the Sabbath, and neglect the house of God; in whose presence you are ridiculing the religion of their parents, and thus teaching them to sneer. It comes to those, let me not call them men, who are mean enough and base enough to teach little boys to swear, and to be obscene; who laugh at the little fellows mouthing their mighty oaths, and retailing with engaging, but to one who loves them, distressing archness, the low slang they have learned in the bar-room and grocery.

It has long come with earnestness amounting to agony, from the drunkard and the drunkard's wife, to the men who have their living by the craft of tempting to every conceivable crime, the poor slave of a depraved appetite. They have long treated this prayer with contempt. It comes to them no longer. But men and women of the state of Indiana, it comes to *you*, louder and wilder than it ever fell before upon mortal ear. The poor drunkard, with all the elements of a noble soul within him yet, though shattered sadly by the assaults of intemperance, comes and begs you, with such entreaty as might move the "pain'dst fiend below" to keep this deadly, bewitching poison out of his sight, and give him a fair chance to be a man again. His wife, who has clung to him through all his downward career, and clings to him yet more closely as others begin to desert, lifts her pleading face. His children, frozen in the very flush of youth into cold, heartless, spiritless things, not daring to look happier children in the face, join their shrill cries, and laying hold of you with their little withered hands, as you rush on in the mad career of party strife, in such a chorus of wo as earth never heard before, they cry out to you, "You have the power, Oh, do not lead us into temptation; put your foot on this traffic, and crush it out of existence." You cannot hear them. The syren of party sings too delicious a song in your ears. It is all well enough to help the poor miserable wretches; but there is some other great project with which they must not interfere; they can wait till next year. The roar of artillery, and the voice of rejoicing that celebrates the success of your favorite measure, will drown out of your ear the wail of the tempted. You cannot hear them, but God can hear them. He will arise, not only for the passionate cry, but even for the sighing of the needy. His ears are always open, and I turn to him: "Holy Father, let them not be led into temptation. Do thou come to their help, for thine is the kingdom, and power. And when this cursed traffic is driven from the land, thine shall be the glory, forever and ever. Amen."

SERMON VIII.

But deliver us from evil.—Matt. 6 : 13.

THE origin of evil has been a fruitful subject of dispute. The philosophers and theologians of every age, have perplexed themselves in regard to it. The only possible solution of this problem, at least in our present condition, is that given in our Confession of Faith: that "God was pleased, according to his wise and holy counsel, to permit" it, "having purposed to order it to his own glory."* It would have been better for multitudes who have disquieted themselves with speculations on this topic, if, content with thus resolving all their difficulties into the ultimate fact of the Divine permission, they had been more solicitous to discover the means of avoiding and removing evil.

Evil is in the world, and it cannot be always eluded. "It must needs be that offences come." No prudence, however thoughtful, no care, however unwearied, can deliver us fully from the consequences of the fall, whether they come in the form of physical or moral evil. What, then, is

* Conf. of Faith, Chap. 6, Sec. 1.

it best for us to do? Shall we cast off fear, renounce the guidance of reason, and resolve to avoid no danger, because we cannot escape all? Every one must see the folly of such a course. Yet this is the logic of some reckless people, who refuse to take any precaution, because all precautions are at times unavailing. They will not have any care of their health, because men are sure to die; or they have known some persons very prudent and watchful on this point, and they were sick as often as any one. There are many parents who seem to act upon this principle in regard to their children. They let them run in the street, and associate at will with the evil-minded and the vicious, making no effort to restrain them. And when remonstrated with, their answer generally is, that it is impossible to seclude children entirely from such influences. I am sometimes tempted to think that argument is thrown away upon such people. Ought they not to see, at a glance, that the fact that evil is so general and inevitable, is only an additional and more urgent reason why we should use forethought; for the more prudent we are, the less we shall suffer.

But shall we, on the other hand, make this certainty of encountering evil in some of its forms, the ground of a refusal to put forth any activity? Shall our prudence degenerate into cowardice?

It does with some people. They will not ride after a horse for fear it will run away. They will not cross the lake or the ocean—nothing could tempt them to—lest they should be drowned. They will not travel on a rail-car, for fear it would run off the track. Now the proper course is, as any plain, common-sense man will tell you, to take all reasonable precautions, and then do whatever is necessary or desirable to be done. Do not pick out a wild horse, and an unskillful driver. Do not put to sea in a rotten vessel, or on a stormy night, or trust yourself knowingly to a drunken engineer. The folly of this excessive timidity appears, from the fact that it often exposes persons to much greater dangers than they avoid. You may always travel on foot, if you think that the safest; yet a tree may be blown down on you, or a mad dog bite you, when perhaps, if you had been travelling in some other, and as you think more dangerous mode, you would have escaped them. And of one thing you may be sure, you cannot, with all your care, escape every evil. You may never see water beyond your depth; yet the fire may burn up your house, and burn you up in it. Wherever you are, you are environed with danger. What can you do, but, after having exercised all proper care, commit your ways unto God?

Some of you, who will think this very good

logic in regard to the things of this life, and who constantly act upon it in relation to them, will yet demur to it, when applied to our spiritual interests. But let us see how it will work. You refuse, my impenitent friend, to do anything toward making your peace with God, for fear you will not succeed. You will not start on the road to heaven, for fear you will never get there, notwithstanding great and precious promises are given unto you to encourage you: "Come unto me, all ye that are weary and heavy laden, and I will give you rest." "Him that cometh to me, I will in no wise cast out." Yet you think we ought to put forth our activity in the things of this life, though God has never given us, either in his word or in his providence, any similar assurance of success. And do you lessen your spiritual danger by refusing to do anything? Do you not rather increase it? Do you not make your destruction certain? Consider the great difference between you and those who are so timid in regard to worldly affairs. They may escape injury by staying at home—they may live a long and peaceful life. The only thing they will lose, may be a little sight-seeing, for which they will be more than compensated by the solid happiness of dwelling among their own people. But you, by staying away from Christ, are certain to be destroyed. You lose everything and gain nothing.

A little froth instead of the river of the water of life; a paste diamond or two for the pearl of great price; a few tinsel toys for a crown of gold. Oh! how can you be so foolish. Will you not say,

"I can but perish if I go,
I am resolved to try;
For if I stay away, I know
I must forever die."

And you, who refuse to make an open profession of your secret hope in Christ, because your hope is so weak, and you fear you will dishonor God, your folly is but little less. Is your faith likely to be strengthened by being smothered? Is the friend, who, though not able to do much, yet defends and assists you, of any less value or credit than he who herds with your enemies, and is silent when you are abused? That dangers beset you is true, but Christ has made you many promises. "Lo! I am with you always, even unto the end of the world." "No man shall pluck you out of my Father's hand." You are not to be presumptous. Do not tempt the Lord your God; do not expose yourself unnecessarily, because he has given his angels charge concerning you. "But watch and pray, lest you *enter* into temptation; and whenever he sees fit to lead you into it, his arm will protect, his eye will watch over you.

I presume you are all convinced of the necessity of forethought in the affairs of this life. But did it ever occur to you that going to God with this petition, "Deliver us from evil," is one of the first dictates of mere worldly wisdom. I assert, without hesitation, that he who lives a prayerless life, however prudent he may think himself, is of all men most careless. He neglects the only sure precaution against an infinite variety of evils. You cannot, prayerless man, as you must see, know what miasma may lurk in the air; or if you did, you could not protect yourself against it. You are utterly ignorant what disease may be engendering within you, even now. You cannot tell in the morning what accidents may lie between you and the setting sun. Danger, disease, and death lurk all along your path, and every foot-fall may bring you into some hidden snare. How soon may disease, disgrace, or infamy worse than death invade your family circle. How wise, then, in you to pray this prayer, if you believe in a God who can protect, and who will hear you! And who does not wish so to believe? Would you not rather adore a being who knows our frame, and *remembers* that we are dust, than one who sees

"With equal eye, as God of all,
A hero perish, and a sparrow fall;"

who will pay no regard to your entreaties, and

will not even be touched with a feeling of your infirmities? And how much better that you should go forth to your daily toil trusting in God, rather than in blind chance or good fortune. Is there any comparison between the two, as a source of patience and strength? "Our rock is not as their rock, even our enemies themselves being judges."

Do you not begin to regret your irreligious life? I might have some hope that you could be persuaded to ask God to deliver you from these physical and social evils to which we are all exposed; but feeling as you now do, it would be idle to urge you to pray to be delivered from sin, at once the worst of evils, and the source of all others. Partly because you think you can deliver yourself, but chiefly because you do not consider sin any evil. There seem to be two stages in the life of an impenitent man; one in which he considers sin a mere trifle, the other in which, though somewhat aware of his guilt and danger, he still thinks he can save himself. Not but that these two feelings run into and modify each other. He who has any proper idea of the evil of sin, never would think of trying to deliver himself. And one reason why men are so contented in their sin, taking no pains to understand its naturo and extent, is, that they imagine they can secure their own safety whenever they do set themselves at work. Still I think these two states may be found in the life of almost every irreligious person, separated by more or less definite limits. Most of you, I apprehend, are in the first of these stages. Sin is no evil from which you wish to be delivered. You would not like to commit any great crime, not because it is a sin against God, but because you would forfeit the respect of your fellow men, or your liberty or life. If the standard of human law or public opinion should change, you would conform to them, even in violation of the law of God. Indeed, you do so even now. Punishment may seem an evil, and in order to avoid it, you may be willing to forego some enjoyments, from which you now derive much pleasure. But once convince you that you could still retain them without any risk of being punished, and you would never think of abandoning them. Some of you may even have taken up this belief, and have, as a consequence, allowed yourselves in many things which you know, and everybody knows, God has forbidden. This shows that sin, in itself considered, is no evil to you. I think it more than likely, that if the cholera were in our midst, many of you would in the morning ask God to deliver you from it; or, if such a prayer were offered up in your presence, in your hearts you would say amen to it. But the leprosy of sin is in our midst, and you are every day exposed to it; yet you never think of asking God to keep you from it; and when you hear such a prayer, you do not respond to it.

Such, my brethren, is not the Christian's feeling. To us, sin is the body of death, and we cry, "who shall deliver us from it?" There is nothing in our religion to keep us from asking our Father in Heaven to keep us from temporal evil. Nay, we have the highest encouragement to do so, for we have the promise of this life, as well as of that which is to come. But let us never forget the infinite superiority of the unseen and the eternal. Let us ever say to "the bounteous Giver of all good,

> "Thou art, of all thy gifts, thyself the crown;
> Give what thou wilt, without thee we are poor;
> And with thee rich, take what thou wilt away."

The doctrinal teaching of this petition is the counterpart of the third: "Thy will be done." In that, we confessed our inability as of ourselves to do the will of God, and asked that his strength might be made perfect in our weakness. In this, we acknowledge that we are unable to resist temptation, and we beseech him to deliver us; to provide us a way of escape. In the petition immediately preceding the one we are now considering, we show that being distrustful of ourselves, we are not greedy of temptation. In this, in praying to be delivered from evil, we not only confess that we are unable to defend ourselves, but remind ourselves that we cannot always avoid temptation; and, indeed, that we ought not to. The mere fact that there is danger in our path, is not always a sufficient reason for a refusal to go forward. Do not let your caution degenerate into criminal cowardice. God may make it your duty to go into the midst of great dangers, both spiritual and temporal. He may surround you with bitter enemies, and cause you to meet with fierce opposition. Many of his chosen people have thus been tried. Beware of being a spiritual sluggard, saying, "there is a lion in the way." Remember that God is able to succor them that are tempted, and will, with the temptation, provide a way of escape.

I remarked to parents, in a former Lecture, that as they could not always keep their children under their own observation, they ought to pray to God not to lead them into temptation. I would remind you now, that even their Heavenly Father will sometimes suffer them to be tried; and you, therefore, need to ask him to deliver them, at such times, from evil. How can you think of all the snares to which their rashness and inexperience must expose them; of the multitudes who make shipwreck of this life, to say nothing of the life that is to come, without being driven to cry mightily to God in their behalf.

Oh, prayerless father and mother, I know not whether to think you more foolish or hard-hearted. You will not ask God, who alone is able, by his Almighty power, to protect and defend your child from all peril and harm, both of soul and body. You are shocked at the atrocious cruelty of those heathen, who carry off their aged parents into the wilderness and leave them to die. But you, more cruel than they, expose your children to every evil influence the world can exert upon them; thus making certain, so far as you can, their eternal death. If you will not pray for yourself, I beg you to pray for them.

"It is better for the children, and for all connected with them," said a parent to me not long since, "that they should die in early life." I cannot think so. It is better, so far as we can see, that they should die young, than that they should live to be miserable or vicious. It is sad to think into what a fiendish expression the placid face of the child may one day be distorted; how bloated that soft cheek, how dull and leaden that bright eye may become. Far better to hide them away in an early grave; to give them up in infancy, to Him who will carry them in his bosom, and suffer no stain to soil them, than to keep them for the doom of the drunkard or the profligate. But is it not still more desirable that they should live to be useful and happy, the honor and support of their parents, a pleasure and a blessing to all who know them? There is many a modern mother, I am persuaded, with her *Gracchi*, who could not think it better always for children to die young. Did the mother of George Washington think so? Would any of you, if God should count your child worthy to put him into the ministry? No prayer seems to me so proper to be offered up for children, as the request which occurs in what is called our Lord's intercessory prayer. "I pray not that thou shouldest take them out of the world, but that thou shouldest keep them from the evil." Who could kneel down at the bed-side of his child, and pray that it might die? Who so hard-hearted, so impious, that he would not pray that it might be kept from the evil. At the same time, if children die in infancy, or early life, we should consider that they are taken away from the evil to come.

It may seem to some who have heard these discourses, that I am an officious intermeddler, in speaking so often and so plainly of the duties of parents to their children. As I shall not have occasion to refer to this subject soon again, let me vindicate myself here against any such captious objectors. The obligation of parents to train up their children in the fear of the Lord is enforced in both the Old and the New Testaments, with great plainness and frequency; and though many have out-grown the wisdom of Solomon and Paul, I still think they had the Spirit of the Lord. I am to keep back none of the counsel of God, and there are many reasons why the duty of parents to watch over and pray for their children, should, least of all, be neglected in the teachings of him who is set over you in the Lord. Our blessed Master commends the lambs of the flock, with peculiar emphasis, to the watchful care of his under-shepherds. It was the first duty which he enjoined upon his repentant disciple. I should be false to him who has put me into the ministry, did I not, upon this very point, reprove, rebuke, and exhort, being instant in season and out of season. And as a watchman on the walls of Zion, charged on the peril of my own life to warn the inhabitants of the land, when I see danger approaching, I feel that I must speak at the present time in no uncertain tones. The Presbyterian Church has, if I may use such an expression, leaned with all her weight upon her baptized children. We have looked to them to replenish our ranks; and though occasionally strangers have taken up their abode among us, and have always been welcomed, yet generally we have drawn our recruits from those who were born within our gates, and have been trained up in our midst. Instead of the fathers, these have been the children. We have always honored family religion; we have laid great stress upon dedicating children to a covenant-keeping God in the ordinance of baptism. We have insisted upon family worship, and the regular instruction of children at home by their parents; and to all these, under God, we owe much of our prosperity as a Church.

But I fear that now we are being shorn of our strength. It is not that the children of the Church go elsewhere. That would not grieve us so much, though we prefer to have them in the home of their fathers. But they go nowhere, save only with the enemies of the cross of Christ. The land is full of lamentations over the scarcity of candidates for the ministry, and various causes have been assigned for this. May not one great reason be found in the decay of family religion? Every one has heard of Madame Campan's laconic and oracular reply to Napoleon's question as to what France required to make her a great nation—"Mothers." The Church wants mothers, mothers who will pray with and for their children, "lead us not into temptation, but deliver us from evil."

It has *always* been the peculiar glory of our Church, that her children were well-governed, and thoroughly taught. Is not this fast degenerating into an idle boast? We seem to resemble some old Highland clansman, or Spanish grandee, who lives on his long pedigree, and the fame of his ancestry; too proud to toil, too indolent to win a name for himself. For while we still hold fast to our ancient boasts and professions, we are practically sinking to a level with those who avowedly, and of conscience, exercise no control over their children, and give them no instruction. It is to be feared, that as we have been exalted so high, we shall yet sink into a lower deep; and as we have been so famous for our faithfulness, we shall grow into a wider proverb for our sad and wicked carelessness.

Do you say there is no ground for these fears? How many households, think you, are there, connected with this Church, that are gathered together every Sabbath, as they were in olden time, to study the Catechism and the word of God? How many that send to the Sabbath-school and the prayer meeting a slim and infrequent representation? How many that are represented in the street on the Lord's day? These are questions which it pains me to ask, and would pain me to answer. Yet there can be for us no surer sign of desolation and decay, than to see the children of the Church not trained up in the way they should go, or departing from it. All our learned ministry, our wealth and intelligence, the impenetrable logic and Scriptural truth of our doctrines, cannot save us, when once these foundations of family government and instruction are out of place. When I see the slightest tremor in this bulwark of our Church, I must cry aloud and spare not. I know I am not your enemy, and I do not believe you will think me so, because I tell you the truth.

The text, "deliver us from evil," will bear another interpretation, which many eminent critics are inclined to give it. The article occurs in the original, and this part of speech is never insignificant or unnecessary in the Greek. A strict translation of the passage would be, "deliver us from the evil;" by which, many say, we are to understand the Evil One, or Satan. The ancient fathers all understood it as referring to him, though their belief in the agency of evil spirits was much more earnest and practical than is fashionable now. A passage precisely similar, and translated in the same way in our version, is that portion of our Lord's intercessory prayer, which I have already quoted. "I pray not thou shouldest take them out of the world, but that thou shouldest keep them from the evil;" and this also many critics interpret of the Evil One. In Matt. 13: 19, and 1 John 2: 13, the same expression occurs in the original; and it is in both cases translated in our version, "the wicked one." In the case of the text, it is proper enough for us to adopt either translation. That is to say, we may pray to God to protect us from the various evils to which we are exposed, or we may ask him to deliver us "from the crafts and assaults of the devil." There are many who laugh to scorn this latter idea, for they do not believe in the existence of any such being. They scout the notion as an exploded superstition; a remnant of the fables of the dark ages. To settle the controversy between them and us, let us betake ourselves to that sure word of prophecy, which still shines amid our boasted civilization, as a light in a dark place.

We are told in the history of Job, that Satan came before the Lord and accused that good man of selfishness and hypocrisy; and that Job was, in consequence, given up to Satan to be tempted and tried. But some say this whole book is an allegory. Where are the marks of its being allegorical? Why not receive it for what it appears upon its face to be; a plain, simple account of what actually happened. But they say it is impossible that such a transaction should ever have taken place. How do they know that? Let them prove it. The Bible is intended to reveal to us what we could not otherwise discover. Who shall say that the curtain is not here drawn aside, and we permitted for a moment to see what is constantly taking place in the presence of God?

only confess that we are unable to defend ourselves, but remind ourselves that we cannot always avoid temptation; and, indeed, that we ought not to. The mere fact that there is danger in our path, is not always a sufficient reason for a refusal to go forward. Do not let your caution degenerate into criminal cowardice. God may make it your duty to go into the midst of great dangers, both spiritual and temporal. He may surround you with bitter enemies, and cause you to meet with fierce opposition. Many of his chosen people have thus been tried. Beware of being a spiritual sluggard, saying, "there is a lion in the way." Remember that God is able to succor them that are tempted, and will, with the temptation, provide a way of escape.

I remarked to parents, in a former Lecture, that as they could not always keep their children under their own observation, they ought to pray to God not to lead them into temptation. I would remind you now, that even their Heavenly Father will sometimes suffer them to be tried; and you, therefore, need to ask him to deliver them, at such times, from evil. How can you think of all the snares to which their rashness and inexperience must expose them; of the multitudes who make shipwreck of this life, to say nothing of the life that is to come, without being driven to cry mightily to God in their behalf.

Oh, prayerless father and mother, I know not whether to think you more foolish or hard-hearted. You will not ask God, who alone is able, by his Almighty power, to protect and defend your child from all peril and harm, both of soul and body. You are shocked at the atrocious cruelty of those heathen, who carry off their aged parents into the wilderness and leave them to die. But you, more cruel than they, expose your children to every evil influence the world can exert upon them; thus making certain, so far as you can, their eternal death. If you will not pray for yourself, I beg you to pray for them.

"It is better for the children, and for all connected with them," said a parent to me not long since, "that they should die in early life." I cannot think so. It is better, so far as we can see, that they should die young, than that they should live to be miserable or vicious. It is sad to think into what a fiendish expression the placid face of the child may one day be distorted; how bloated that soft cheek, how dull and leaden that bright eye may become. Far better to hide them away in an early grave; to give them up in infancy, to Him who will carry them in his bosom, and suffer no stain to soil them, than to keep them for the doom of the drunkard or the profligate. But is it not still more desirable that they should live to be useful and happy, the honor

Who shall say, when a servant of the Lord is stripped and tormented, as is sometimes the case, that the devil is not at the bottom of it? I think he often is. And even supposing, as most persons do, that what is said of Satan coming with the sons of God, &c., is merely a figurative representation, it is certainly designed to teach us the existence of the Evil One, and his agency in our temptations and troubles. There are other passages of Holy Writ, which express the same truth in a similar way. Zechariah saw in his vision, (3: 1.) "Joshua, the high priest, standing before the angel of the Lord," that is Christ, "and Satan standing at his right hand," where the accuser always stood in the Jewish court. The apostle John heard a loud voice, saying in heaven, "Now is come salvation, and strength, and the kingdom of our God, and the power of his Christ, for the accuser of our brethren is cast down, who accused them before our God, day and night.

But granting that all these passages are figurative, though I think there is more reality about them than is generally supposed, what will you do with those places in which the devil is said to be a liar, a murderer, and the like? In this we are told by an apostle, the children of God are manifest, and the children of the devil. Is the devil a mere abstraction, a personification? Why then may not God be also? And it may be shown to be, just as logically, and in the same way that the devil can be. Take this passage in the third chapter of Habakkuk:

"God came from Teman, and the Holy One from mount Paran. His glory covered the heavens, and the earth was full of his praise. And his brightness was as the light; he had horns coming out of his hand; and there was the hiding of his power. Before him went the pestilence, and burning coals went forth at his feet. He stood and measured the earth: he beheld, and drove asunder the nations; and the everlasting mountains were scattered, the perpetual hills did bow."

Now there is much more reason to say that this passage is allegorical, than the one in Job. It occurs in a highly wrought poetical book, with not a single historical statement in it; nothing at all resembling the staid and quiet narrative of Job's life and employments. The language is evidently figurative; the transaction never could have actually taken place. Why may I not say that the word of God is a mere personification; that wherever it occurs, and in whatever way it is used, it is never to be understood as designating any really existing being.

What folly to reason thus, if indeed it can be called reasoning. And why are they guilty of such absurdities, when they find such passages as the following: "The angels who kept not their first estate, but left their own habitation, he hath reserved in everlasting chains, under darkness, unto the Judgment of the great day." "Depart, ye cursed, into everlasting fire, prepared for the devil and his angels" To do away the certainty of future punishment, they must annihilate the Evil One, and so fly in the face of plain and repeated declarations of the word of God. Be not deceived, my brethren. The Scriptures reveal to us the existence of one, to whom, under the various names of Satan, the Devil, the Evil One, the Serpent, the Dragon, the Adversary, they ascribe the same general qualities.

It is a singular fact, that those who are most skeptical as to the existence of such an evil spirit as is revealed in the word of God, have been the readiest to take up with the wild and foolish delusion of spiritual rappings. They could not credit the plain and repeated declarations of the Bible, but they could put unlimited confidence in the unsupported assertions of men and women of doubtful sanity, or questionable character. They could not believe that the devil had anything to do with our most distressing afflictions, or the direst calamities; yet they do not hesitate to declare that "the departed spirits of the mighty dead" engage in moving tables, and writing school-boy compositions. So true is it, that infidelity naturally leads to superstition.

But suppose there really is such a being, is there any reason why we should pray to be delivered from him? Is he anything more than a bugbear to frighten naughty children with? Yes, my brother, he is your enemy and mine. Our Lord tells us expressly, that the enemy is the devil. The apostle Peter calls him our adversary, the devil. The word Satan, by which name he is often designated, means an adversary. He is called in the Revelation of John, the accuser of the brethren. He is everywhere represented as opposed to us, seeking our ruin. He first seduced us to the foul revolt, and ever since he has labored for our destruction. Many professed Christians have no real, hearty belief that the devil is their enemy. I can remember distinctly when the conviction first forced itself upon me that *he hated me*,—that he watched for my halting, and when I faltered, obscure and unknown though I was, he and his followers raised a shout of triumph. Now this is not a fiction, a figure of speech, it is a reality; and he who does not feel it to be so, is not aware of one of his greatest dangers. And this is but a fulfillment of the oldest prophecy on record. "I will put enmity between thee," said God to the infernal serpent, "and the woman, and between thy seed and her seed." We are the seed, the spiritual children of him who is to bruise the serpent's head. We must expect to be assaulted by the serpent in turn.

And he is not an enemy to be despised. He was once a mighty angel, in the presence of God, and he is still powerful.

> His form has not yet lost
> All its original brightness, nor appears
> Less than archangel ruined, and the excess
> Of glory obscured ; as when the sun, new risen,
>
> Looks through the horizontal misty air,
> Shorn of his beams.

Darkened so, yet shines the fallen archangel. He is called in the Scriptures the Prince of the power of the air; and this is a Hebraism for the powerful prince or ruler of the air. In other passages he is said to be the god of this world; thus teaching us his power. There are also in the world evil spirits ; and though the word of God reveals nothing definite in regard to their number, their names, and their employment, and we venture on dangerous ground, when we dogmatize on these points; yet we are expressly exhorted to put on the whole armor of God, because we wrestle not against flesh and blood, that is, with mere earthly enemies; but against principalities, against powers, against the rulers of the darkness of this world, against spiritual wickedness in high places, or, as some translate it, against wicked spirits on high; this last expression corresponding to the phrase, the prince of the power of the air. I do not think it idle or superstitious to repeat the warning. The caution has not grown obsolete. Such foes are in our midst, and, for aught I know, millions of these spiritual wickednesses walk the earth, or when we wake, or when we sleep. They are said to be the angels, the messengers of that Evil One, from whom our Lord teaches us to pray to be delivered. He is called their prince. He can station them where he will, to watch and waylay us. Shall we not, then, call upon God for protection?

The devil is a bold enemy. He disputed with Michael about the body of Moses, that chosen servant of God. In his vision in the Isle of Patmos, the beloved disciple saw him and his angels fighting in heaven itself, with Michael and his angels. And though these passages are obscure and mysterious, still they show the boldness of our enemy. We do know that he crept into the paradise of God, and tempted the mother of all living. He had the presumption to venture into the presence of Jehovah, and to accuse the upright Job of serving God from selfish and hypocritical motives. And above all other instances of his audacity, he assaulted our Lord, who was holy, harmless, and undefiled. He would have had him, who is the brightness of the Father's glory, and the express image of his person, who sits at the right hand of God, to fall down and worship the dethroned and faded spirit who dwells in the blackness of darkness forever. Shall we hope to escape? Do you think you can daunt such a bold, sagacious enemy, by assuming an air of defiance, and by asserting, with school-boy bravery, that you are not afraid? Can you flatter yourself that you are so pure and virtuous that Satan, feeling how awful, simple goodness is, will not venture to tempt you? And do not think that these are idle questions. Multitudes have had this self-confidence, and have been ruined by it. I warn you against it. You must resist the devil, if you would have him flee from you. Remember that he tempted our Lord, that angels fell by him, and pray to God to deliver you from him.

The devil is a subtle and crafty enemy. We are told of his wiles and devices. We are fore-warned lest we fall into his snare. We are told that he transforms himself into an angel of light; that his coming is with all power, and signs, and lying wonders. Good old Matthew Henry says, he is called a serpent for subtlety; an old serpent, experienced in the art and trade of trapping. Paul bids us beware, "lest by any means, as Satan beguiled Eve through his subtlety, so our minds should be corrupted from the simplicity that is in Christ. And it is not alone the Christian that he attacks. He blinds the minds of them who believe not: lest the light of the glorious Gospel should shine unto them. When men hear the Gospel, then cometh the devil and taketh away the word out of their hearts; lest they should believe and be saved. And thus they are taken captive of him at his will. Do any of you, whether religious or irreligious, suppose that you can yourselves circumvent or elude this crafty foe? Ah! you do not know "the depths of Satan." The gayest, most attractive places you see, are often the snares and pitfalls he has prepared for you. The sweetest music, the softest tones you hear, are often the syren song with which he would lull you to sleep, that he may rob you of your soul.

The devil is a savage, bitter enemy. He goes about like a roaring lion, seeking whom he may devour. He is a serpent, venomous, spiteful and hateful. He is an unscrupulous enemy. Our earthly foes may revolt from some modes of warfare, but there is nothing which the devil is not mean enough and base enough to do. He is a liar and a murderer, from the beginning. He is a slanderer: witness what he said of Job. In some parts of our version of the New Testament, the same word is at one time translated the devil, and at another, slanderer. The latter is the original meaning, but it was so appropriate to our great enemy, that it came to be used as his proper name. Indeed, in the book of Revelation, he is expressly called, by those who are in heaven, the accuser of our brethren, who accuses them before God, day and night! There are those in every community who are constantly, day and night, hunting up and repeating stories of the knavery and hypocrisy of ministers and professors of religion; insinuating, or broadly asserting, that their piety is but a cloak for their profligacy and dishonesty.

Do these men know who they are imitating,—of what lineage they come? Our Savior said to just such false accusers, "ye are of your father the devil, and the lusts of your father ye will do." My friend, if you must be in the employment of the Evil One, do not, I beg you, do his dirty work. Do not let him use you to spatter filth on those who are trying to live godly in Christ Jesus.

I have intimated that some men are in the employ of the adversary. Harsh as it may seem, this must be applied to every one who is not a servant of Christ. Our Lord tells us there is no neutral ground; he that is not for me, is against me. And yet, though he employs you, my impenitent friend, he is your enemy still; he gives you only the wages of sin, which is death. He does not now assume an attitude of opposition. He gives you "the pleasures of sin for a season," but it is only for a season. He acts like a gambler or seducer. He toys with you as they do with their victims, that he may get you under his power. When he has rifled you of all you hold dear, he will turn you out to everlasting shame and contempt; as his prime ministers on earth are doing with their victims every hour.

If you had such an earthly enemy as I have described, bold, wary, vindictive, powerful and unscrupulous, would you not dread him, and seek to be delivered from him? Is Satan any the less to be avoided, because he is a spiritual foe,—because himself unseen, he wars against your unseen and eternal interests? Ah! if he had not already blinded your mind, you would seek to recover yourself out of his snare.

My Christian friends, while all this will seem to the irreligious and the giddy a fable or a delusion, to you it is, I am persuaded, a sad reality. The devil hates us as he hated our Master, because we are not of this world, and he shows his spite against us. He fills our minds with evil thoughts. He dresses up sin in an attractive garb. He excites unreasonable and wicked men to insult and provoke us. Let us not underrate this enemy. There is often, among Christians, a light and easy way of speaking of our adversary, which is very improper. Not that I think the devil ought to be treated with any reverence. Some good people seem to have the same scrupulous respect for him that they have for the Almighty. They think it as great an evidence of a wicked heart for a man to speak thoughtlessly of the devil, as to blaspheme that glorious and fearful name of the Lord our God. But, on the contrary, it is comparatively the most guiltless kind of profanity, if, indeed, it can be called a profanation. I feel as free to speak of the devil as of a wicked man, and I do not think any more regard should be paid to him. But beware of acting and talking as if there were no such being, countenancing the popular idea that the belief in his existence is an exploded superstition of the middle ages. That, "in this enlightened age," we have nothing to fear from him, and that nobody but nursery-maids and bigots believe there is any such creature.

No, my brother, it is still as true now as it was in the days of the apostle, that your adversary, the devil, goeth about like a roaring lion. You must resist him steadfast, in the faith. You must put on the whole armor of God, and fight manfully the good fight of faith. You are, above all, to take the shield of faith, that is of trust in God. You are to rely upon him, praying always with all prayer and supplication. All these passages show you that all your safety is to be in praying this prayer: Deliver us from the Evil One.

"Man's wisdom is to find,
His strength in God alone;
And an angel would be weak,
Who trusted in his own."

SERMON IX.

For thine is the kingdom, and the power, and the glory forever. Amen.—Matt. 6 : 13.

THIS conclusion contains the reason why we should ask of God what we need, and why he should give us what we seek. It shows the propriety of our coming to him, and of our coming to him with just such requests. In the first place, the kingdom, the authority, belongs to him. He is a Sovereign ; none can stay his hand, or say unto him, what doest thou ? Every page of the Bible contains this truth, either expressed or implied. "The Lord hath prepared his throne in the heavens," says the Psalmist, "and his kingdom ruleth over all."* "The Most High ruleth in the kingdom of men, and giveth it to whomsoever he will. And all the inhabitants of the earth are reputed as nothing, and he doeth according to his will in the army of heaven, and among the children of men.."† "Shall I not do what I will with mine own.‡ "He hath mercy on whom he will have mercy, and whom he will, he hardeneth."§ And even those who attempt to evade the force of these plain declarations by subtle arguments,

---

* Ps. 103 : 19. † Dan. 4 : 17. ‡ Matt 20 : 15. § Rom. 9 : 18.

and acute criticism, when they come to pray, address our Heavenly Father as a sovereign. They do not ask him to help them to get what they need, but they entreat him to give it to them; thus recognizing him as the *giver* of every good and perfect gift; the God in whose hands our breath is, and whose are all our ways. So you see that in our devotions, both reason and conscience respond to the truth of this great doctrine, so plainly revealed in the word of God. Indeed, it is only on the basis of this doctrine, that there is any place for such prayers as every pious heart offers, and feels compelled to offer to God. If he is not a Sovereign, if he does not do what he will in the army of heaven, and among the children of men, why should I ask him for anything with such an unconditional submission to his will, when my dependence upon him for it is only remote and indirect, if, indeed, there is any such dependence at all?

Surely, those Christians, who in words deny and argue against God's sovereignty, (and by this I mean his most holy, wise, and powerful governing of all his creatures, and all their actions,) surely, cannot know to what their reasoning necessarily leads. Hear the language of one, who, denying this doctrine, and not having any piety to keep him from being consistent, has dared to follow out this denial to its legitimate results. "In what prayers do men allow themselves. That which they call a holy office, is not so much as brave and manly. Prayer looks abroad, and asks for some foreign aid to come, through some foreign virtue, and loses itself in endless mazes, of natural, and supernatural, and mediatorial, and miraculous. Prayer, as a means to effect a private end, is theft and meanness. It supposes dualism, and not unity in nature and consciousness. As soon as the man is one with God, he will not beg." And again he says, "Mens' prayers are a disease of the will."*

I know that many, who dispute God's sovereignty, will shrink with horror from such blasphemous sentiments. And I am far from supposing that the pantheism of the expressions I have quoted, is a legitimate deduction from these principles; but I think the denial of the usefulness of prayer is. I see no other stopping-place, when once you refuse to acknowledge that his kingdom ruleth over all.

We hear much in our country about popular sovereignty. Now this is all well enough, if we do not mean thereby to dispute the sovereignty of God, or to endorse that vicious and blasphemous saying, "the voice of the people is the voice of God," thus enthroning the multitude,

---

* R. W. Emerson.

the majority, in the place of God. He who denies that there is any law higher than the constitution or other supreme law of the land, puts into the hands of the constituted authorities, the power to obliterate the eternal distinction between right and wrong. He opens the door for the most unlimited despotism. He denies the sacred right of revolution. Especially in a republican government, where the will of the majority makes and alters constitutions and laws, is there no other reliance for the safety of the minority, and the individual, except this much abused, much misunderstood doctrine of a higher law, this great truth that God alone is a sovereign in his own right,—that the sovereignty, even of the people, is but a delegated sovereignty, and to be exercised only within certain limits; and that when it transgresses these limits, our allegiance to God should absorb every other feeling, should break every other tie.

And lest it should be said that this authorizes every one to nullify any and every law of the state, at his own caprice, I would remind you that this very higher law itself, binds us to be subject to the powers that be, because they are ordained of God. And when any one refuses obedionce to the law of the state, he must prove from the same law, which enjoins obedience in all ordinary cases, that there is a conflict between the pect the Almighty to operate, so as to grant us our requests, while at the same time he leaves us a sure basis for action and reasoning, by not suffering our experience to be contradicted or interrupted.

But let the great apostle of this doctrine, Dr. Chalmers, speak for himself: "Instead of treating it as a general argument," he says, "let us take some individual examples. When the sighing of the midnight storm sends a fearful agitation into the mother's heart, as she thinks of her sailor-boy, tossed on the tempestuous deep, the advocates of a hard and inflexible constancy in nature would forbid her to pray. According to them, prayer to God, who holds the elements in his hand, is as useless as to the elements themselves. Yet nature strongly prompts her aspirations for the safety of her boy, and, if our argument be true, there is nothing in science to repress them. God can answer her, not by interfering with second causes, or reversing the changes of the heaving atmosphere; but by a touch of his hand amid the deep recesses of meteorology. Thus he might bid the elements into silence. A virtue passes out of him, which passes onward from the invisible to the visible."

It would help to clear away the mist in which this whole subject is involved, if men only had a clear idea of what a law of nature really is. We may say of this idol of modern skeptics, what Paul did of those of the ancient heathen: "We know that it is nothing in the world." A natural law is a mere statement of the order which we have observed in the succession of events. For instance, you say that it is a law of motion, that action and reaction are equal. What more do you mean by this, than that it is universally true, that the action of one body upon another is always succeeded by an equal reaction? What more do you know of the efficient cause of this succession, than he who never heard of this law? The only advantage you have of him is, that when you see one body come in contact with another, he may discover that in that specific case, action and reaction are equal. But you know that it is always so, and you can take advantage of this general principle to avoid danger, or to accomplish what you desire. But as to what makes it so, you are both equally ignorant.

Take another illustration, for men are slow to learn that in their investigation of natural laws, they do not discover a single really efficient cause, but simply establish, or rather ascertain, an invariable order of events. I see an apple fall to the ground. I ask you why it does this, instead of moving in the opposite direction, or floating around in the air? You say, the earth attracts it. Is this anything more than merely repeating

that it actually does move toward and to the earth. I ask you what makes the earth attract it, and you say it is the law of gravitation that makes it. What is this law of gravitation but a simple statement of what has been proven to be universally true, "that all matter in the universe tends toward all other matter." Do I know any more *why* the apple falls to the ground after I have been informed that this single instance is but a specimen of what is going on constantly all over the universe, than I did before? These laws of nature, which men idolize, are only the uniform modes in which God ordinarily exercises his power. If he saw fit, he could act on an entirely different method, as he has done occasionally. But he has seen fit, in his wisdom and kindness, so to conduct the affairs of the world, that we know, as men say, what we can depend upon. It would be a sad affair if we did not. Now I say again, that we who pray to God, do not ask him to interrupt this regular, orderly succession of events. We think he can answer our prayers without doing that, though we have no doubt, if the occasion demanded it, he could, and would, vary from his ordinary method of governing the world.

I have, as you will remember, repeatedly called your attention to the sound philosophy of this prayer. It may not be out of place to remark here, that the whole word of God, while it does not, and was not intended to, give direct instruction upon any subject but religion, yet its teachings are based upon, and harmonize with, the deductions of a correct mental science, and, indeed, of all science. That is to say, it does not tell what sort of a being man is; it does not go into any analogies of the powers and affections of his mind. But in all it says, to or of him, it goes upon the supposition that he has just such faculties, and it is adapted to a being possessing just such faculties, as we know man to be actually endowed with; thus showing that, like the Sabbath, it was made for man. And so, though a correct philosophy is not directly inculcated in the word of God, it is always involved in its teachings.

Even here, in this conclusion of the Lord's prayer, there lurks a great metaphysical truth, to which every profound thinker has set the seal of his approbation. They tell us that power is an attribute of the mind. And though we sometimes ascribe it to inanimate matter, that this is but a mere figure of speech. We speak of the power of the wind or the sun, but this dead, lifeless matter, is merely the instrument of some mind.

We are not, on this account, to abandon the use of such phrases, any more than we are to stop saying that anything made a deep impression on our mind, or that a new idea struck us. But we are not to be deceived by these expressions. We are to remember that whenever we see power, there is evidence of the presence of mind.

This may seem absurd to some of you, but it is the received doctrine among metaphysicians, and I will show you that it has the endorsement of one whom you will confess to be a man of sound practical wisdom. Dr. Noah Webster, in his definition of the word power, says "the exertion of power proceeds from the will; and in strictness, no being, destitute of will or intelligence, can exert power." See, now, how this idle, empty abstraction comes in to second the teachings of our Lord.

There is nothing in this prayer at which men of the world would be so inclined to sneer, as at the idea of asking God for daily food. Why, they say, the wind, and the sun, and the rain, these great natural agencies, will ripen your grain for you; you need not trouble the Almighty about it. But philosophy rises up and says, the wind, and the sun, and the rain are mere lifeless matter; they can only be the instrument of some mind. The Bible tells us who that mind is; it is God, who gives us all things richly to enjoy. He makes the sun rise, he sends rain, he holds the winds in his hand. How proper that we should say, "Give us this day our daily bread, for thine is the power."

But man has will and intelligence, therefore we may properly speak of his power. Yet man is evidently a limited, dependent being; his power must be derived from some higher source. This is what mental philosophy teaches. Need I ask you how this accords with what the Bible says of God's power? God hath spoken once, says the Psalmist: twice have I heard this, that power belongeth unto God. That is, he is the only being who has underived power; and he is, therefore, the fountain of all power.

When Pilate told our Lord, "Knowest thou not that I have power to crucify thee, and have power to release thee," our Lord answered with philosophical accuracy, if I may use such an expression, "Thou couldest have no power at all against me, except it were given to thee from above." We here ask God to do for us, and for our fellow men, what we are ourselves to do; such as hallowing his name, doing his will, &c., because our strength to do these, in the most comprehensive use of the phrase, must be derived from him. Especially, (and I would not, in the general truth, lose sight of this particular phase of it,) must a disposition to do these things, which is an essential element of our power, be born, not of the will of man, but of God. What a motive to induce us to ask our Father, who seeth in secret, is this blessed truth, that all power in heaven and earth is in his hands.

The last reason given here why God should hear our prayer is, that it will be for his glory. This has always been a favorite plea with the obedient children of our Heavenly Father. "What shall I say, when Israel turneth their backs," said Joshua, when they had been routed by their enemies, "for the Canaanites, and all the inhabitants of the land, shall hear of it, and shall environ us round, and cut off our name from the earth, and what wilt thou do unto thy great name?" "For thy name's sake," said the Psalmist, "pardon mine iniquity." And again, "For thy name's sake, lead and guide me."

Even our Savior prayed, "Father, glorify thy Son, that thy Son also may glorify thee." This is the great plea which we should urge before our Heavenly Father, why he should answer our request. He tells us expressly, "them that honor me, I will honor;" and he declares he will not give his glory to another.

If, then, you would have your prayers answered, you must plead with God to hear you for his own name's sake. And in order that this plea may be acceptable and available, it should be the great motive which induces us to ask such things of our Father in Heaven. Whether we eat or drink, or whatever we do, we are to do all for the glory of God.

If, then, we pray for daily food, for life and health, it should be that we may glorify God. We should say with the Psalmist, "For in death there is no remembrance of thee, in the grave, who shall give thee thanks?" If we ask to be forgiven, our great motive must not be our own safety, but that our salvation may be to the praise of the glory of God's grace. With David we must say, "There is forgiveness with thee, that thou mayest be feared; that is, reverenced." And, "For thy name's sake, pardon my iniquity." If we pray that we may do the will of God as it is done in heaven, it should not be that men may call us honorable, but that seeing our good works, they may glorify our Father who is in Heaven. And so I might go on with every petition, showing that the reason why we should ask, as well as why God should answer, is, that he may be glorified in us.

We learn also from this doxology, that praise should always form a part of our worship. We may say that this prayer begins and ends in praise; for the first petition, "Hallowed be thy name," may be viewed in the light of an ascription. The Bible is full of precepts and examples, which show that it is our duty thus to glorify God. "O! that men would praise the Lord for his goodness, and for his wonderful works to the children of men."—Ps. 107: 31. "Let us come before his presence with thanksgiving, and make a joyful noise unto him with psalms."—Ps. 95: 2. "By him, therefore, let us offer sacrifice and praise to God continually; that is, the fruit of our lips giving thanks to his name."—Heb. 13: 15. "Whoso offereth praise, glorifieth me."—Ps. 50: 23. The prayers of many good people are sadly deficient in this respect. They are full of giving thanks to him for all his mercies; humble confession of sin, both original and actual; earnest supplication for the pardon of sin and peace with God, and for all temporal mercies that may be necessary; and of intercession for others, including the whole world of mankind.

But there is little "adoring the glory and perfections of God, as they are made known to us in the works of creation, in the conduct of providence, and in the clear and full revelation he hath made of himself in his written word." Yet this should always be adverted to in our prayer, especially in public and family worship, and should be often made a prominent topic. The advantages of such a course are many. It impresses upon the worshipers a sense of the majesty of the being whom they address. It shows that he who leads their devotions, is aware what a solemn thing it is to address the King of kings. And it is an important duty thus to praise and glorify our Father in Heaven. Many people suppose that all these ascriptions are to be confined to spiritual songs. But there are multitudes who never sing. Shall they never praise God with their own voices? Besides, many of our hymns and prayers, earnestly entreat for some great blessing. These two departments of worship are separated by no well-defined limit. He who sings, as I have remarked in a previous discourse, should feel that that exercise requires a devout spirit, and forbids all jesting and frivolity, equally with prayer. He who prays, should not come to God merely as a beggar, but as an adoring worshiper. Let your prayers often ascribe dominion, and power, and glory to our Father in Heaven.

The word amen is from the Hebrew, and is either a form of acquiescence, as, "Let it be so;" or, of aspiration, "May it be so." It may be considered as applicable to this doxology which we have just been considering, or to the whole prayer. As related to the former, it teaches us that we are not merely to believe that the kingdom, the power, and the glory are God's; but we are to wish that they may be, and to rejoice that they are. When we pray to God, we ought not even to feel,—surely no one would dare to say,—"Lord, thou canst do as thou wilt, for thou art supreme; thou canst do what I ask of thee, for thou hast all power; thou wilt get all the glory, therefore thou oughtest to grant my requests. But if I could, I would help myself, and get all the honor to myself. I come to thee, because I am obliged to." No, the language of our hearts should be, "Let it be so. I am willing thou shouldst have the dominion, might, and honor. Nay, more, so would I have it. Oh, that it may be so." And why should it not be a source of joy to you, that no one can control the Almighty, while he can do whatsoever he pleases? Why should you be restive and unhappy, when you think of God's supreme dominion? Why should you try to prove that he has not so much control over you, and your actions? One would think that you ought to rejoice, that all power is in the hands of such a wise and merciful being.

Can you think you would be happier, if left to your own short-sighted guidance, and impotent protection? Only have the Almighty for your friend, and you are safe. You may dwell at ease. You can say to every shadow o'er your path,

"Whatsoever thy name may be;
  Whithersoever thy coming tends;
Or if my pathway passes thee,
  Or at thy fated station ends,
Thou knowest what 'tis thou bring'st to me;
  I know who 'tis that sends."

Instead of thinking this belief in God's sovereignty a creed of fear, it seems to me the only sure ground for the patience of hope. I say with the Psalmist, "Oh, Lord God of hosts, blessed is the man who trusteth in thee."

It has never occurred to me that it was necessary to prove that God intends to have, and will have, all the glory of everything he does for us. But there may be some doubters, and even cavillers here; and a few plain passages of Scripture will set the matter at rest. The apostle Paul, in speaking of God, says, not only that all things are by him, but that they are for him. We are told in another place, that the Lord hath made all things for himself.

The Psalmist, in speaking of the deliverance of the ancient Israelites, says, the Lord saved them for his name's sake.

Ezekiel, in speaking of the return of the Jews from the Babylonish captivity, represents the Almighty as saying, "I do not this for your sakes, O house of Israel, but for my holy name's sake, which ye have profaned among the heathen whither ye went." "Neither hath this man sinned," said our Lord of him who was born blind, "nor his parents; but that the works of God might be manifest in him." And over and over again, in every variety of form, we are told that the salvation, of which all other deliverances are but the type, and compared with which they are but as the setting to the precious stone, is of grace, that it may not be of works; that boasting may be excluded; that no flesh may glory in the presence of the Lord; that our adoption may be to the glory of his grace. I need add nothing to such declarations as these.

Now it has always seemed to me more difficult for a large class of men to consent to let God have the glory, than anything else they are called on to do. A love of honor is not "the last infirmity of noble minds" alone. All men are inclined, more or less, to seek the honor that comes from man, and with some, this is the greatest obstacle to their salvation. You see so many who will not pray, because this is an implied acknowledgment of our entire dependence upon God, and that the glory of everything belongs to him. There are such multitudes who are hoping to be saved by their good works, who will not take salvation as a free gift, that God may be glorified; who will not unite with the Church, because that is a public, open recognition of the fact that God is to have all the glory. Now if the Scriptures are true, and the word of God cannot lie, if reason, too, is not deceitful, you see that the power is all of God, and that, therefore, he ought to have the glory. Would you seek to deprive him of it? Shall a man rob God? Will you not render to him the glory due unto his name? Even if you cannot rejoice that it is so, can you not be honest enough to say it is just, it is right, let it be so? And, Oh! if you had but a glimpse of the infinite goodness and loveliness of our Heavenly Father, you would not only say, I am content, but you would rejoice and bless God, that the glory was to be his forevermore; willing to be but a little unnoticed ray, in the effulgence that surrounds the throne of the Eternal. Is an affectionate child jealous and envious of the greatness his father has achieved, which reflects honor upon him? Is he restive and dissatisfied when he sees that all he does, is ascribed to the judicious counsels and the careful training he has received from his parents.

This is, I know, "to compare great things with small." But it is something like a representation of what our feelings toward our Heavenly Father should be. And when you love him with all your heart, it will be your greatest source of pleasure, that God is to have all the glory. Even here below, you will sing that song of the ransomed, "blessing, and honor, and glory, and power, be unto Him that sitteth upon the throne, and to the Lamb, forever and ever." And as you near the home of the blessed, and hear this song swelling up from the multitude whom no man can number, in the fullness of your soul you will cry out, Amen, and amen.

This closing word may also be considered as applied to the whole prayer, thus deliberately re-affirming and setting our seal to all that we have said. It is thus we generally employ it, and it ought not to be used lightly and irreverently. There may be, and I presume there often are, prayers offered up, which are so faulty, that we would be constrained to dissent from them. Few prayers fall from the lips of uninspired men, every expression, every sentiment of which we could approve. But who cannot say amen to this prayer our Lord taught us ? Go read it, this sweet Sabbath morning, to the bloated drunkard, the trembling debauchee, the rude swearer, the fierce, quarrelsome man of violence. Let them give in their verdict. Will they not say, never man spake like this man ? Take it around to every household in this place Are there any fathers or mothers, however wicked, who would refuse to have their children taught it ? If our Lord had brought us no other message but this prayer, that would have been a mission worthy of a teacher sent from God. Mother, teach your child this prayer. Though prayerless yourself, let those whom God gives you, be accustomed, from their very infancy, to call him their Father in Heaven; to trust in and obey him as such.

Such another talisman, in all time of peril and adversity, earth cannot afford. Whatever else you may give them, whatever else you may leave them when you die, bequeath to them this trust in God, for it is a pearl of great price, for joy whereof they might well sell all that they have and buy it. It is an anchor to the soul, both sure and steadfast, entering into that within the vail.

My Christian friends, there are some of you, whose homes I fear are unblessed with the sacred influences of family worship. I pity you. Tell me, you who find so many excuses for neglecting this delightful duty, for refusing this unspeakable privilege, could you not learn this prayer our Lord left on record for us? I knew a mother, a widow, with helpless little children, dependent upon her, who gathered her household band around her every day, and together they audibly repeated the Lord's prayer. I have heard them, and it seemed to me, that I stood in one of the sweetest and holiest spots on earth. Oh! widowed mother, go thou and do likewise; for if any children need the protection of this Heavenly Father, it is such as yours. And what I say unto you, I say unto all, commend yourselves, and your loved ones, morning and night, to Him to whom the darkness and the light are both alike.

I would not be guilty of any idolatrous reverence for the mere words of this prayer. But it comes home to me with an overpowering influence which I can never express, yet cannot conceal. Our Lord often prayed alone. What mortal shall ever dare to plead as did our Master then, when he poured out his soul with strong crying and tears? Inexpressibly dear as is his intercessory prayer to every believer, much as I thank him for having prayed it, and left it on record, there are yet expressions in it which must not fall from merely human lips. But here is a prayer our Lord teaches us; it is fitted to us, to our weak, frail, blinded condition, at once brief and comprehensive. One may learn it in a few leisure moments, and yet within its narrow compass, it unfolds everything that we need, both for this life and that which is to come. Awful, yet at the same time tender; for while it hallows God's name, and adores him as king, it yet calls him Father, and asks him for daily bread. So simple that a child can receive it, so profound that a philosopher, nay, an angel may lose himself in its depths. I love to repeat it. When I hear this prayer amid the solemn worship of God, it seems to me a low sweet prelude of the music of heaven. Even snatches of it, sound upon my ear like the faint and far-reverberations of that new song, which is ever singing in the presence of God.

I know not how I can better conclude this series of discourses, than by gathering up the fragments of this prayer, which we have been so long considering, and repeating them as one united whole; for standing alone in its simple, unapproachable grandeur, it is its own highest eulogy.

Our Father, which art in heaven, Hallowed be thy name. Thy kingdom come. Thy will be done in earth as it is in heaven. Give us this day our daily bread. And forgive us our debts, as we forgive our debtors. And lead us not into temptation, but deliver us from evil. For thine is the kingdom, and the power, and the glory, forever. And let all the people say, AMEN.